THE
Vermont
Ghost
EXPERIENCE

Conjured by
Joseph A. Citro
&
Robert Waldo Brunelle, Jr.

Eerie Lights Publishing
Eerielightspublishing.com

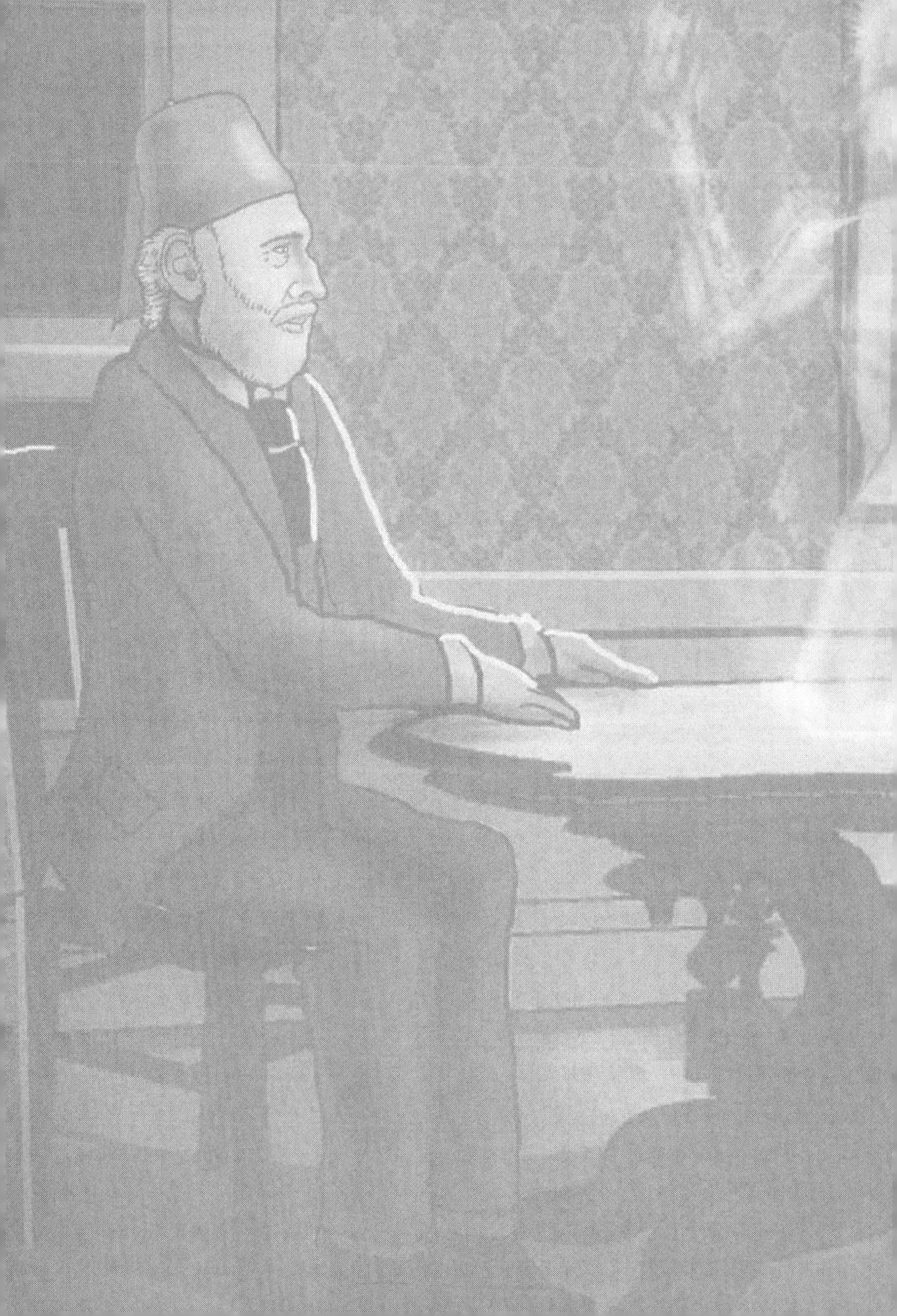

The Vermont Ghost Experience

Conjured by

Joseph A. Citro
&
Robert Waldo Brunelle Jr.

ISBN 978-1-945950-25-4

EERIE LIGHTS
Eerie Lights Publishing
Eerielightspublishing.com

Edited by: Jerry Hajewski

Book layout/design: SMAK
www.smakgraphics.com

Also By Joseph A. Citro
From
Eerie Lights Publishing:

The Vermont Monster Guide
with Stephen R. Bissette

The Vermont Ghost Guide
with Robert Waldo Brunelle Jr.

Contents

PART ONE

Introduction: What Are These? 1

The Richford Horror 15

The Cotton Mill Ghost 25

The Dutton House 35

The Griswold Murder House 43

St. Albans 56

PART TWO

Introduction: The Night Visitor 69

The Jews of Middletown 73

An Awful Story 87

Extro 103

About the Creators 113

"The earth hath bubbles, as the water has,
And these are of them."

–Macbeth I,3

PART ONE

INTRODUCTION

What Are These?

No matter where you live, it is likely that within a twenty-mile radius, someone is being plagued by inexplicable ghostly activity. Some people suffer in baffled silence; others summon the authorities, the clergy, or the media. In such uncertain circumstances all make a giant step toward accepting what they had always considered unbelievable.

And each will have a story to tell....

For more than twenty years I have been collecting Vermont's true tales of the unusual, the baffling, and the macabre. By far the majority of them have been ghost stories.

In this book artist Robert Brunelle and I will take you on a tour through some of our ghostly neighborhoods. There we'll introduce you to the resident spirits and point out the homes in which they dwell.

Along the way many questions will come up again and again. Chief among them, experience tells me, will be this: If there really are ghosts, why do they stick around?

Good question!

The short answer is, we simply don't know. After 200 or more years of earnest psychic research, we still don't have a clue. Certain people say ghosts stay behind to complete some unfinished business. To deliver messages. Or to exact revenge on someone who wronged them in life.

Others think ghosts are unreasoning fragments of once-living personalities. That a moment of great passion or great pain can imprint an image that – when the conditions are right – will repeat itself over and over, like an endless loop of videotape.

Some people suggest there is some undefined relationship between haunt and habitat – that the dead attach themselves to a

1

much-loved property, in some cases not even realizing that they're dead.

And then there are those who insist that ghosts are the result of intersecting dimensions, that someone, or something, can exist then and now, there and here, all at the same time.

Bottom line: Who knows? We could get stuck on this single question and never progress beyond this book's introduction.

It seems to me that ghosts, like living people, have a limited lifespan. There are long-forgotten ghosts that used to pester our ancestors, but now seem to have blinked entirely out of existence. Who or what were they? Alas, we'll never know.

Of course, the same thing is true of documented ghost stories. (By "documented" I simply mean that they have stepped out of the oral tradition and onto the page – that accounts have been written down somewhere, by someone, sometime.) These tales, like the literary bestsellers of yesteryear, experience their flash of ghostly glory and are gone, unknown entirely to the next generation of book buyers... or ghost lovers. Historians like Ohio's Chris Woodyard have filled volumes with forgotten ghostlore resurrected from long out-of-print newspapers and journals. (See her *The Face at the Window* and *The Headless Horror*).

Of myriad ghost stories – documented and undocumented – what interests me is why some catch on and some do not. For example, there is Emily and her bridge in Stowe. She is without a doubt Vermont's most heralded haunt. In fact, last time I consulted Google, she had received 815,000 hits.

Though Emily supposedly died around 1850, we didn't hear much about her till 1970 or so. Dead, yes, but far from gone. Today people flock to her bridge hoping to get a glimpse of the dear dead girl. She has become a celebrated supernatural superstar.

In Emily's case the alchemy was inevitable. There's the romantic setting of a covered bridge. And the backstory involving a teenaged girl committing suicide after she is jilted just before a midnight rendezvous. Emily's supposed ghost lives on like a vampire, taking her sustenance from generations of curiosity seekers, ghost hunters, and paranormal investigators who learn and spread her story.

So why don't other events, equally poignant and dramatic, produce ghosts? Or at least ghost stories?

A perfect case in point might be Waterbury's "House of Light."

The House of Light

Long before Hurricane Irene brought merciless destruction to Vermont, we were not in the habit of naming storms; they were free to wreak their havoc anonymously. Perhaps the most devastating weather in Vermont history will always be known simply as "The 1927 Flood." The state has never fully recovered. The cruel events were the inspiration for H.P. Lovecraft's one Vermont-centered horror story, "The Whisperer in Darkness." And the damage survives to this day, in dramatic photographs, movie footage, and living memory.

The deluge happened over a three-day period, November 2 through 4. So much rain saturated the area that the ground simply could not absorb another drop of water. Yet rain continued its deadly descent; waterways overflowed, sewers backed up, and roads turned into rivers. People fled the rising tide by climbing to the upper stories of their houses, then to the rooftops.

And the downpour continued. The relentless waters took out more than 1000 bridges, decimated miles of roads – dirt and blacktop – and washed away the supporting ground beneath railroad tracks. Modest homes and stately mansions were destroyed. Buildings collapsed. Eighty-four people died, including the state's Lieutenant Governor S. Hollister Jackson.

The town of Bolton was entirely cut off by the flood waters, with no way in or out. People tried to keep afloat using anything they could, from wooden doors to empty coffins. An eyewitness, Deputy Sheriff Howard Todd, recorded pitiful scenes of family members bidding one another farewell as they died in the water.

Local newspaperman Lloyd Squire reported, "We had our hands pretty full right at the moment saving our own lives and as many others as we could."

In a cruel kind of irony, flood conditions were especially bad in Waterbury. There citizens endured more than their fair share of distress, destruction, and death. The Winooski River rushed through town, chewing away its banks and toppling structures too weak to resist its onslaught. By nightfall of the second day, some people feared that Waterbury and the whole Winooski Valley would be swept away.

But Lloyd Squire and those around him were about to witness something more unsettling than the rising, rushing tide.

Mr. Squire told the tragic story of John Jerome May, his wife, and four children. Unable to flee their home, the family made their way to the attic, huddling together, praying for help, trembling at what this terrible night might hold in store.

Eventually, above the cacophony of the storm, they felt a tremendous shudder and heard a thunderous crack. An earthquake, they thought, as in an instant, the whole structure broke away from its foundations and began floating down the river. Terrified, the Mays clung tighter to one another, awaiting their fate.

On-site, reporter Squire picks up the story of the runaway house as it bobbed and lurched through town, swept along by the brutal surges of a river out of control. "It went very quickly," Mr. Squire wrote, "and though some said they could distinguish figures moving past windows, nobody could tell for sure whether the house was occupied during that wild ride.... But it very likely was. If it had been a house from which the occupants had gone before the flood came, the lamps would have been turned out."

It is difficult to picture the human drama and the surreal horror of what was going on. The night was made darker by the curtain of rain continually pouring from the cloud-thick sky. The shouting of townspeople could barely be heard against the roar of the rushing Winooski. Stumps, full trees, buggies, and livestock churned along, half seen in the mighty caldron of water.

And suddenly, unbelievably, the massive hulk of a house floated into view like an ocean liner in distress. The light from kerosene lanterns glowed eerily from every window, surrounding the place with a kind of mystical halo.

Heart-breaking screams of children issued from inside.

Selectman William Agan couldn't believe what he saw coming

toward him. As he watched in horror, the form of John Jerome May appeared from inside, clutching the frame of an attic window.

"For God's sake, where are we?" Mr. May cried.

The Selectman shouted back, "You're passing Bill Agan's house."

Mr. May paused, bewildered, then said, "Well, goodbye, Bill, I guess we're gone."

The House of Light continued along its chaotic course in the Stygian torrent. In a matter of minutes Mr. Agan heard a terrific crash. The house and family were no more.

Although the floating house story is absolutely true, it is nonetheless long gone. That surprises me. Today, very few have heard of it. And what surprises me more is that an event of such magnitude did not give birth to any ghosts, or ghost stories, or legends in general.

What I mean is, you'll never hear this around the campfire: "And it is said that on certain chill nights, when the fog hangs thick over the river, people have seen that looming bulk of a house moving slowly downstream, gliding like a hydrofoil just a wee bit above the dark water. They say it gives off an aura, a muted glow, yet no sound can be heard. People gawk at it in stunned silence. And among them, certain people swear to have heard a distant voice, forlorn and tragic, saying, 'Goodbye, Bill, I guess we're gone....'"

So why does one story inspire a ghost tale, while another, equally marvelous, does not? Why do Emily and her bridge have a long lifespan while Mr. May and his floating, phantomlike house have sunk into oblivion?

Such are the myriad mysteries of the spirit world.

Some, however, might say the answer is simple: Houses don't have ghosts because houses don't have souls.

Well, maybe not, but it is an assertion not consistent with the ghostlore of this world. Animal ghosts have been reported. Ghostly doors have appeared and vanished. Phantom trains silently chug along empty tracks. (And I must not forget the Ghost Train occasionally reported in Chittenden, Vermont, that sometimes ventures into thickly forested areas where railroad tracks have never been.)

And houses? My friend Paul Eno, a supernatural sleuth from Rhode Island, tells of what I call "Johnson's Part-Time House." Like Brigadoon, sometimes it's here and sometimes it isn't.

Before I continue with his story, a short introduction to Mr. Eno would be in order. Although he is a prize-winning journalist, longtime editor, accomplished historian, and former seminarian, he has also been investigating the paranormal for more than forty years. In that time, he's come to look at "spirits" in unorthodox ways, and he applies a new vocabulary to related phenomena. As he says, he takes ghost investigation "out of the séance room," and suggests that whatever ghosts may be, they are not spirits of the dead. His opinion of paranormal investigators may be equally irreverent. "With few exceptions," he says, "I find them ridiculous."

I tend to agree with him, which brings us back to houses. Strictly speaking, they are not alive. They never were alive. So, presumably, they can't die. And their walls and roofs and masonry simply cannot generate "spirits" that might evolve into ghosts. Therefore, ghostly houses, like ghosts, must be something other than the spirits of the dead.

Johnson's Part-Time House

Back in the summer of 1974, two land surveyors, Clement Ridley and Bud Harper, were working in the woods near Johnson, Vermont. As their day came to an end, they moved out of the trees and on to an old logging road. It was no great surprise when they eventually saw a good-sized farmhouse – an old one – about a quarter mile away. The place must be deserted, way out here in the middle of nowhere, they thought.

Moving closer, the men remarked on how dilapidated it was... but wait! They clearly saw smoke curling from the chimney... and clothes drying on the line. So, someone was living there after all!

"A bit off the grid," Clem said, puzzlement clear in his voice.

"Yuh, but there's something weird about it," Bud responded quietly.

No vehicles were in the yard. No driveway. No electrical wires ran to the place. Everything about it just seemed... odd. Still, they continued toward it. When they were less than sixty feet away a bearded man came around a corner, carrying an ax on his shoulder. He was slender and wore a broad-brimmed hat. Bud Harper greeted the man, but he didn't seem to hear.

Then Clem Ridley called out. Instead of answering, the man just looked around, kind of confused.

The surveyors wondered if he could be deaf and maybe blind, too?

For some reason – maybe it was the ax – Bud and Clem began to feel uncomfortable. . . and soon left.

Later, still puzzled, they studied their U.S. Geological Survey map. Oddly, the old house was not on it, though normally such maps include all major buildings and houses.

A few days later, after many jokes about government inefficiency and oversight, they returned to the spot.

They were shocked to discover the old house wasn't there. Mr. Ridley said, "There was no sign of it! We didn't make a mistake

7

about where we were – maps don't lie!"

Completely flummoxed now, they hurried to the Johnson Town Hall where town records revealed that yes, there in fact had been an old house at that exact spot.

It had burned down in 1910.

But they had seen it, stood in its dooryard, scrutinized its occupant.

It had been there.

Then it wasn't.

Door to... somewhere...?

Another atypical "ghost" makes its appearance in a story told to me by Mark Massie of Colchester. In addition to Mark, I interviewed two other witnesses: his brother Matt, and their mother. All three tell the same story.

The maternal side of Mark's family came from Scotland during the 1700s and settled in the Ryegate area. There, James Whitehill, Mark's ancestor, built a stone house on his 600 acres. The house still stands; each year it hosts the family reunion.

Mark enjoys many childhood memories of the place. But there are other memories, too: the most profoundly puzzling incident of his life occurred there when he was in his early teens.

I think it is important to note that it happened on a bright summer's day, not during "a dark and foggy night" nor amid the terrors of a thunderstorm.

Mark and his brother Matt were near the house picking and eating wild raspberries. In time they tired of that, so they decided to head out and do some exploring.

They followed the old stone wall on the property line. Then, Mark says, "A few hundred yards away the oddest sight met our eyes... [O]n an adjacent hillside – there in the middle of the hill – was a door!"

Seized by excitement, the boys rushed to get a closer look at the unfamiliar sight. It was, in fact, embedded in the hillside. And, they soon discovered, it was no ordinary door. Mark says, "This was a wood plank door with rough iron bolts and an iron lock which hung on a hasp. The hinges were long and also made of iron attached to a frame of wood.... The door looked... weather-beaten and crude, perhaps a bit intimidating...."

But there was an immediate flash of disappointment: Though they tugged and tugged, the ancient lock held firm.

So off they ran to tell their parents about their strange discovery. Alas, their enthusiasm was short lived. Their mother, who had grown up on the property, recalled no such door and said she thought her boys had been in the sun too long.

Yet Mark and Matt knew what they'd seen, and, after repeated insistence, their mother agreed to take a look... just as soon as she returned from St. Johnsbury, where she had an appointment.

The impatient boys accompanied her as they headed out. Driving past the field in question, all three could clearly see the strange door in the distant hillside.

Mark's mother was completely amazed. She stopped the car to

stare. Then she reiterated that in all her years on the property, she had never seen the door nor had she heard anyone speak of it. Now she too was determined to check it out when they got back home.

Mark recalls, "Our excitement mounted every minute we were away.... We ran all the errands... and then left St. Johnsbury for Ryegate."

But as they drove slowly past the field, they couldn't believe their eyes. The doorway was gone!

Understandably, all three sat in shocked silence. Then Mark and his brother bolted from the car and ran into the field to find their lost door. Surely it could not have disappeared.

They looked high and low for what just a few hours earlier had been plain as day. But after a long and thorough search, no trace of the door could be found.

Mark is sure they didn't imagine it. And to this day he can't imagine what they would have found if they had opened it. And if they'd gone inside, what then? Where might it have led them?

Over the years, on innumerable visits, Mark has been unable to rediscover his vanished door. Yet it exists quite clearly in his memory. It was really there. He has two unimpeachable witnesses to prove he was not hallucinating.

So, what did the three Massies see? The ghost of a door?

I have heard similar stories, but they simply make no kind of sense.

For example, I spoke with a woman from Chittenden with an odd tale to tell. She and her husband were amateur geologists who were fascinated with the rocks in the mountains around their home.

Do Not Enter

One day, hiking quite far from their little town, the couple wandered far off the trail and into an unfamiliar part of the forest. There they found what she described as a small canyon. Its steep walls supported some sparse vegetation; its floor was cluttered with tumbled stones. Looking up, the couple saw what they never expected to see. There, on the face of a cliff, was what appeared to be a rectangular opening.

"What is that?" the woman asked.

Her husband just stared. Then, slowly, he made his way closer. At the same time both realized that they were in fact looking at an opening in the cliff side. Clearly it was manmade. Stranger still, it contained a metal door, partly open.

The husband climbed the cliff as far as the door and verified, yes, it was in fact a metal door embedded in the rock wall. The door was open about a foot and rusted in place, so it could be neither opened more nor closed.

Still, the opening was wide enough to slip inside.

"Wish I had a flashlight," he called back to his wife. Ahh, but he did have matches! He was able to crawl part way through the opening and look around. The interior was tomb black except for the area illuminated by sunlight.

He didn't need to light a match to see a monumentally weird sight that would stay with him the rest of his life. Inside, carved from the stone itself, was a set of stairs, leading downward. It was too dark to see where they might lead.

Though his curiosity was painful, he knew that without lighting and the proper gear it was too dangerous to enter and explore.

Determined to come back with friends and appropriate equipment, the couple headed home, all the while speculating where the door and stairs might lead. What could be down there? And who could have constructed such a thing? Miners, maybe? The military? The door's metalwork appeared far too old to be any sort of cold war relic. And why were there no trails leading to the site? Obviously, no one had been there for a very long time. There wasn't any graffiti, nor litter, nor any indication that the site had been visited for many years.

The rest of the story is not difficult to guess. On several more occasions they tried to find their way back to the spot. And were never able to. Not only were they unable to relocate the door, they couldn't even find the little canyon nor cliff side the door was carved into.

Some years later the husband died without ever solving the mystery.

When I talked to his wife, she was in her 70s and disinclined to hike off into the mountains again. Curious as I was, I felt the same way.

So, our initial question – "If there really are ghosts, why do they stick around?" – isn't really the question we should be asking. In fact, I cannot formulate the question we really need to ask. It is something like, "What is all this stuff that shouldn't be here, but is?"

Ghostly apparitions, phantom houses, ghost ships, fairy doors... and then there's Bigfoot, UFOs, gnomes, banshees, all manner of night bumpers. What of them? Why do none of them stick around? Are they separate, fleeting phenomena? Or different varieties of illusion? No matter. Nothing is off limits. For the purposes of this book, I'll refer to them all, collectively, as The Vermont Ghost Experience.

The final word is this: Whatever they are, they're here. Then they're gone.

And we're left scratching our heads and trying to formulate the proper questions.

Thanks to Jeremiah Chila, Paul Eno, Mark and Matt Massie, and a lady who wishes to remain anonymous.

What Are These?

The RICHFORD Horror

"We didn't know what we were dealing with."

The Richford Horror

There could not be a more classic ghost story. This one has all the elements of a 19th century gothic novel... or a 21st century horror movie. To me, it is nearly perfect.

Events began around 2000 in the tiny northern Vermont town of Richford, right on the Vermont-Quebec border. But this inexplicable episode might as well have taken place on another border: that mysterious, ever undulating line that separates our reality from some other.

You know how it starts. An attractive young couple – we'll call them Laura and Will – were looking to buy their first home, a place where they could settle down and raise their children.

Money was an issue, of course, but they learned about a grand old building that had been on the market for some time – and the price was right. Worth a look, they thought. So, they took a drive to check it out.

At first all they could see was a tower in the distance, but as they got closer and crested the knoll, the whole place was revealed like a snapshot of another era. It was huge, a three-story Victorian. With a tower! Their own tower! For these enthusiastic young parents, it was love at first sight.

The romantic notion of owning such a place perhaps obscured their clarity of vision: the clapboards were falling off, here and there holes penetrated the roof, the front door had been kicked in. Piles of garbage tumbled everywhere. But Laura said, "Oh, it couldn't be this house could it? Naw. They can't mean this house. We couldn't be that lucky."

But that was the house, all right. And to them it was a beautiful vision of their future.

You know how stories like this work, though: Laura and Will, wide-eyed and innocent, just didn't know what they were getting into.

They hurried back to visit their banker. And that's when they got their first surprise.

"Oh, you don't want that place," he told them. Odd, Laura thought. Their credit was good, and bankers were not in the business of NOT lending money. But it wasn't an issue of their credit score; they could have the loan if they insisted. But the banker's advice didn't change. "Don't," he said. "Just don't."

For years not only the banker, but most locals, had been referring to the place as "The Haunted House." Of course, Laura and Will didn't know anything about that. And if they had known they wouldn't care. It was the home of their dreams, unique, potentially elegant; for a while they thought it was the best stroke of luck they'd ever experienced.

Sure, the dilapidated relic had some history, but what old place didn't?

They learned that their Victorian dream had begun life as an Episcopal boys' school, but it had never been finished. The church abandoned their project due to what they said were "enrollment problems." Though the diocese maintained ownership, they never again worked on the building. Renters came and went. Nobody would stay long. Apparently it had been vacant as much as it had been occupied.

"Oh," people would say to them, "So you bought the old haunted house!" And they began to hear the stories, stories they chose to ignore. Because Laura and Will were modern, sensible people, they didn't hold with the notion of spooks. The only thing that scared them was the amount of work they'd have to do on their fixer-upper.

But soon after moving in, things started to happen.

Will and a friend were working in the cellar. Confident they were alone in the house, the guys were joking around, having fun as they worked.

Then...

"Someone's here," Will said. Both men snapped to attention, listening to heavy footsteps tromping above their heads. Too heavy to be Laura's, Will thought, so he put down his tools and climbed the cellar stairs to see who'd come in.

No one was there. He checked all around, calling out to the unknown visitor, "Hello? Who's there?" Will examined the windows and doors: Everything securely closed up and locked.

No one else was in the house.

Will's friend came upstairs to join him in the kitchen. But he didn't help Will look around. Instead, he left. Hurriedly. And he never came back. He knew all the stories about the old place. Now, in his mind, they were true.

The first weekend Laura and the children spent alone in the house; they had their German shepherd for company.

At this point they were completely moved in, but the huge old place was still half-empty. Piles of boxes here and there didn't begin to fill the spacious rooms. Laura looked around, thinking they'd just never get everything fixed up right and proper. The walls needed work. The floors, warped and uneven, needed sanding or carpeting. Everything was–

SMASH!

Something crashed to the floor in the kitchen. The dog jumped to his feet, ears up, head cocked. Not growling or barking, just being attentive, looking in the direction of the noise.

Laura hurried out to see what had happened. The cause was obvious: a bottle had fallen off the top of the refrigerator and landed on the floor. Just one bottle out of many. That's kind of odd, Laura concluded at once, because the refrigerator was tipped slightly backward.

"In order for that bottle to fall off the front of the fridge," Laura told me, "it had to go uphill, across the rubber seals, up and over the door and fall, and that was kind of bizarre."

Bizarre, yes, but not really frightening.

That was to come later...

Laura and her husband became increasingly aware of the many subtle oddities about their new home. Nothing serious, just little things. But then something happened that caused them to reassess the level of danger and to take a new look at the situation they'd gotten themselves into.

The oldest daughter, Dori – always a fearless little six-year-old – began to develop what seemed to be an imaginary playmate. She'd spend long hours alone – or maybe not alone – playing in her room. At night, Laura said, "She'd sleep on one side of the bed to make room for someone else. She was in there very comfortable with the fact that somebody was in there with her."

Laura describes her daughter as, "a girl who'd walk into a bat cave and not have fear. She's never been afraid of anything. Not of the dark, not of anything."

Then one night "she came tearing downstairs... eyes huge, hysterical, almost collapsing she was so scared."

Now Dori said there was something else in her room. Something different.

While lying in her bed, Dori had seen what she could best describe as "a white, cloudy thing" standing near the doorway. It was moving slightly, and the girl watched it until it rushed directly at her. That's when she panicked.

After that the little girl who would fearlessly enter a bat cave refused to go back into her own bedroom.

Now everything had changed. Sure, Laura and her husband knew something was a little off in their new home, but now whatever it was had involved the children.

Their other daughter, Susie, had been frightened of the house from the very beginning. She was never comfortable upstairs, where she'd always be looking around as if expecting something to jump out at her, too.

She had a special box in which her precious "glass things" were packed: figurines, knick-knacks, important stuff to a small child. The box was a foot wide, a foot deep, and about two feet long. And it was heavy!

One night while she was in bed Susie watched that heavy box lift up off the floor. It hovered in the air for a moment. Then it dropped.

She heard it hit the floor, heard her glass things rattle around inside.

Laura soothed her, trying to get her to settle down. She soon became convinced that the little girl had seen exactly what she described: a heavy box lift into the air, remain suspended for a time, and crash to the floor.

Oddly, in spite of the impact, and the noise, none of the delicate glass figurines were broken.

On another occasion Susie saw a bag full of her toys move, unassisted, across the floor of her room. Laura says, "She was so paralyzed she couldn't get out of the bed. She would just stay there and when I would go and check on them throughout the night she would be lying there, terrified."

Both girls explained their fear with such conviction that Laura had no choice but to believe them: Something was regularly floating down the steps from the attic. It passed through the solid door and into their bedroom. Whatever it was, its attention was most certainly focused on the girls!

They showed Laura how, in an effort to defend themselves, they had begun collecting stuffed animals from all over the house and using them to construct a protective barrier around their beds. Their partition was almost three feet high!

She was stunned. She told me, "I don't remember the exact words of what they said, but it was to the effect that [they built the partition so that] when the person comes down the stairs at night and goes through the door, it won't go across their beds. Because it's been coming down the stairs, through the door, and across their beds. And they didn't like it."

"Your house is supposed to be your sanctuary," she continued. "This is my place where we're safe from the outside world, and not only were we not safe from– we didn't know what! We didn't know what we were dealing with."

We can only imagine the intensity of the stress such a series of events would place upon a parent. Not feeling safe. Not knowing if your children are safe. Not being certain that you can protect them. You hope things will get better on their own, but for Laura and her family, everything just got worse. The most frightening event almost caused them to pick up stakes and abandon their "dream house."

For no discernible reason, their seven-month-old boy, Teddie, suddenly took sick. Up until then, Laura says, "He was healthy; he had always been healthy. Not so much as an ear infection or anything along those lines." So it was completely unexpected when the infant started getting warm, then feverish to the point that he became lethargic and began to become limp.

Laura took his temperature, and, she says, "I couldn't even find it. Because I wasn't looking high enough. And I say this – and I'm careful who I do say it to because it almost makes me sound like a fool – but that child had a 106 temperature. I swear he did. It was that high."

She phoned the hospital immediately, and they told her to get the child cooled down at once. She took him upstairs where they hopped into a cool shower together. After that she lay down with him. She looked around at the seemingly empty room. Not knowing what else to do, she spoke, trying to communicate with whatever might be there with them. "If you're here and you can hear me please help, do something. Please help. How can you even be here and witness this and not do something?"

Her pleas seemed to work. "I'm not saying that's the reason," Laura told me, "but his temperature went down. Within a half hour... it was just about normal."

In a long interview, Laura summarized the story thus far. "You have a big house so you can have room and so you can spread out and the kids can go play. It got to the point where we were all huddled together on the first floor. Wherever I was, that's where everybody else wanted to be. Because nobody wanted to go upstairs alone. Nobody wanted to function. And so I was telling my husband, maybe it's time we think about leaving. We might as well live in a shed for all the good this big house is doing us."

Richford is a caring community. A lot of people were concerned about the welfare of Laura and her family. Serendipitously, a nearby neighbor thought she might be able to help. A lifelong Vermonter, senior citizen, and courageous soul, Hazel Pratt wanted to lend a hand in a situation most people would have fled from.

Of course, she knew the building's reputation. She had watched families move in and quickly make an exit. In fact, she had a list with the names of seven families who had tried the house but couldn't tame it. One such family had moved out and relocated only a block away. Apparently, that was far enough.

Before Laura's family could move into "a shed," Hazel had an inspired idea. She had been a successful dowser in the community for more than seventeen years, with a remarkably good reputation for finding water.

She offered to try an experiment: Could she use her dowsing rods to find ghosts? It was the first time she'd ever attempted using the traditional tools of the dowser in that way.

Laura and Will readily gave her permission.

The house was so big and potentially confusing that Hazel wasn't sure where to begin. The best idea, she decided, was to start at the top and work down. It didn't take her long to detect... something.

Hazel has described the dowsing process to me, but it seems to operate on an intuitive level that I simply don't understand. Here's how she explained it: "I have my dowsing rod – when I find their energy field... it almost feels very warm, just like if you bring your hand towards your body at a certain distance you'll feel that warmth. It's the same thing when I use my rod. I put it close to the edge of them [the ghosts] and just start asking questions."

Through careful question and answer, Hazel eventually was able to determine who the ghostly squatters were... or had been. She discovered that there were two entities in the house, two brothers. They had been living there, in spirit form, for a long time. The one who stayed in the attic, was – in death as in life – a shy, retiring soul. But the other was more aggressive; he roamed through the house at night. He liked to look in on the children, and in doing so, scared them half to death.

Hazel, using the link established by her dowsing rods, talked to the brothers, one at a time. A gentle and persuasive soul herself, Hazel was able to coax them to leave. "Now just reach up" she told them, "and we'll help you go."

And they were gone!

Although this tale unfolds much like many other traditional ghost stories, at least it has a happy ending. I have talked with everyone in the narrative (except the phantom brothers) and have visited the house on several occasions. To me, much is left unexplained. But that, I suppose, is the nature of supernature. It is, by definition, a mystery.

NOTE: Although the names have been changed for privacy, all quotations reproduce the actual words of the people involved.

The COTTON MILL
Ghost

*"As the great machine had flung the thing it had killed aside,
Mahoney caught the shape of it out of the tail of his eyes,
and he knew that it was a woman."*

– Canton Repository

The Cotton Mill Ghost: A Historic Haunt

The night of June 29, 1900, was dismal and dark.

As the Central Vermont Flyer chugged northward toward the city of Burlington, the wind picked up, smashing a nearly impenetrable curtain of rain against the glass of the cab. The engineer squinted into the darkness, hardly able to see the tracks ahead. He blew the whistle and rang the bell as the engine approached a crossing just south of Burlington Station. After a few more nearly unendurable minutes he would be able to relax a bit while passengers boarded the cars before continuing the run to Montreal.

But the storm made him late; he was way behind schedule.

The time was 6:40.

It couldn't get any darker.

Three young women hurried across the green at Lakeside Park, a small complex of worker houses built by the nearby Queen City Cotton Mill. Like the train, the girls too were running late, rushing to get back to work before the bell rang. In fact, it had already rung, its toll lost amid the storm's ferocity. If they were speaking at all it would have been in French, for all three youngsters were from Quebec – Marie, her sister, and a friend.

It is possible they heard the train. The bell rang and the whistle shrieked as the monstrous locomotive approached. But being young and spry and perhaps a bit foolish, they dashed in front of it. Two made it safely across. But something happened to the third. Maybe she stumbled. Maybe her skirt caught on a railroad spike. Maybe the rain blinded her, or the wind knocked her off balance. Quite possibly she was simply too slow.

In any event, the massive engine struck her, sending her body seventy-five feet through the air, killing her instantly.

But the big news was yet to come.

Nearly forgotten now, this story about the collision of a train and a girl launched a chain of events that is spectacular in Vermont ghostlore. The whole strange saga was revealed in a series of articles in the Burlington Free Press during 1900 and 1901.

First, on June 30, 1900 (pg 5), they reported the death of a 22-year-old French Canadian laborer named Marie Blais (pronounced Blay), but they got her name wrong, calling her Mary Blair. The railroad's own account called her Masie Blair. This confusion may be indicative of the way French Canadians were regarded in Burlington at the time. They were lowly laborers and little more.

But despite her social status, Marie Blais was about to receive an extraordinary amount of attention.

Though she was most assuredly dead, people began to report encountering her in the area where she had been killed. Her ghostly form was spotted near the tracks, around the tenement houses in Lakeside Park, even within the cotton mill itself. Workers would occasionally spy her wan specter, with its strange, fixed stare, watching them as they labored at their looms.

Then, at night, watchmen reported her transparent outline hovering around the machinery. Others saw her, glassy-eyed and pale, wandering aimlessly about the workplace.

That fall frequent appearances of Marie's ghost drew crowds of hopeful spectators to the Cotton Mill where witnesses continually recalled strange noises and assorted unsettling phenomena.

According to reports, hundreds of people saw the phantom. In fact, her many appearances made ghost-hunting a popular pastime for Burlingtonians. And, as all accounts suggest, searchers were rarely disappointed.

About a year after Marie's death, she was still making her presence known. On May 8, 1901, the Free Press said her ghost had appeared again near the lake. Crowds of ghost hunters quickly assembled along the shoreline.

Extremely scary details became associated with the story. For instance, people repeatedly heard a paralyzing wail near the spot where Marie had died. Its source could never be determined.

Phantom obstructions appeared on the tracks, then vanished when the train had slowed or stopped. Some nights the engine's headlight mysteriously failed in the vicinity of the crash.

And Marie would unfailingly appear to the same engineer, at the same spot, every time he drove the train north from Rutland. Supposedly her ghost harassed the poor man so relentlessly that he eventually had to quit his job.

Anyway, the story of Marie Blais's death and supernatural reappearance spread so persuasively that crowds flocked to the spot night after night. But in time Marie failed to meet them.

After a time, she was never seen again.

And then forgotten entirely....

Exactly why ghosts appear for a while and eventually vanish forever remains a mystery. And it is odd that the strange sad saga of Marie Blais has so thoroughly disappeared from local memory, while less spectacular ghostly tales live on.

Why does one ghost go and another stay?

Well, no one really knows, but in this case–considering the disembodied shrieks, phantom obstacles, and failing headlight – it might seem as if Marie were trying to get the train to slow down as it passed the fatal spot.

One possible explanation for Marie's departure came several years after her death, in 1908. Over the years the dangerous crossing where she died had also taken a number of other lives, including at least one child. Hundreds of workers crossed the tracks four times a day – morning and evening, and also for lunch – just as the Rutland Express zoomed by.

For fear of more train-pedestrian collisions, the railroad finally got around to attacking the problem by installing an elevated bridge at the spot where Marie had met her end.

Now people could enter the factory by way of an underpass, so no one ever again had to set foot on the railroad track.

That bridge is still there today... so perhaps Marie doesn't need to be.

AUTHOR'S NOTE:

This story has tremendous charm; after all, who doesn't like a pretty girl, a railroad train, a grisly death, and a ghost? But details become a bit clouded with various intrusions of reality and unreality.

Whatever may be "true" or "untrue" about Marie and her ghost, the tale was pure gold for yarn-spinners of varied types: storytellers, fiction writers, and newspaper editors desperate for copy.

I'm sure it would be impossible to track all of this ghost's oral and literary descendants, but it was treated as fiction at the very same time it was being reported as fact. And printed as fiction in *The Burlington Free Press*, the very newspaper that first broke the story as fact! On November 12, 1901, they published a fictionalized version by Lilian Wright of Westfield [Vermont] in which Burlington becomes Blankton, French-Canadian becomes Irish, and Marie becomes Kathleen.

Ms. Wright's fiction also appeared in a Maine paper. And,

my friend Chris Woodyard points out, the tale was printed as far away as Ohio in a greatly modified form by the *Canton Repository* (December 24, 1905). Apparently, they ran it as a traditional Christmas ghost story.

This time Burlington remained Burlington, Marie remained French-Canadian, but she became Josephine Ladue instead of Marie Blais.

Confused? Of course you are! And such is the nature of the supernatural tale.

Most of us just dismiss it all with a shrug while thinking, there must be a grain of truth in there somewhere. And that is generally good enough. A ghostly tale has its own truth, I think, and it may have nothing to do with actual historical events.

ADDITIONAL INFORMATION:

Just for fun, and as an example of how a "true" tale can morph, here is the way our Vermont story appeared in the Canton Ohio Repository on December 24, 1905. Many thanks to Chris Woodyard for tracking this down.

You might give some thought to which version you prefer...

GHOST OF A GIRL GUARDS CROSSING

Dead Girl Haunts the Place
Where She Was Killed.

Mystery of Vermont Road Engineer of Limited
Which Caused Her Death

Meets Fate in Collision Near Spot
Where Fatal Accident Occurred.

Boston.

This is a story of a factory girl's ghost, which has been haunting a matter of fact, superstition-hating New England community for two years. It is a ghost that many God-fearing folks swear they have seen, and their reports of the shadowy shape have made the whole of commercially centered, unimaginative, cotton-manufacturing Lakeside, on the outskirts of Burlington, Vt., believe it.

It was in the spring two years ago that Josephine Ladue received employment in the Queen City Cotton company mill at Lakeside.

Whence the girl came nobody knew. From the beginning there was a shadow of mystery on Josephine Ladue. She had no relatives in Lakeside nor anywhere else so far as anybody was able to learn. She lived alone. She did not mix with the women and girls of the mill and none of them ever knew her to permit any man to press his attention to her. She had a happy, care-free, sympathetic disposition and she had a smile that rippled forth infectiously.

Josephine Ladue had been at the Queen City less than two months when she disappeared. Whither she went nobody knew, and when she took her place at the looms a few days later she didn't consider it necessary to enlighten anybody as to her movements. A week after that the girl dropped out of sight again, and the whispering which had started with her first appearance grew in volume and point.

These mysterious comings and goings of Josephine Ladue continued with periods varying from two weeks to a month between them. Her qualities as a worker had been the thing that stood between her and being discharged. Finally, her example began to bear fruit in the ranks of her fellow workers in broken discipline and disregard for the regulations governing the employees of the Queen City mill.

Josephine Ladue was warned that if she ever went away again from the mill without being excused, she need not return.

It was only a week later that the girl, defying the warning she had received, disappeared. Three days later, she was back, and the foreman told her her place had been filled.

"You can't send me away," she threw at him. "I'm going to work at these looms, and at seven o'clock tonight, when you have all gone home, I'll be at my looms."

The girl's words mystified the foreman.

That evening as the village hall bell was ringing out seven o'clock big Denis Mahoney, at the throttle of the Rutland railroad's Burlington flyer, reeled through Lakeside, southward bound. He knew he was on time, but from force of habit he looked up from his cab window at the clock on the Queen City Mill. For an instant his eyes were held by a girl in a window working deftly at a loom. The light in the mill was so bright that he saw every feature plainly. He saw that she was good-looking, and he noticed, too, that her lips were parted in laughter.

Mahoney brought his eyes back to the singing rails ahead and in that moment, something happened – something that had happened to a good many engineers before him and to many since – something that had often been described to him, and he knew as he caught his breath what he had done. As the great machine had flung the thing it had killed aside, Mahoney caught the shape of it out of the tail of his eyes and he knew that it was a woman.

31

When the flyer's engineer brought her to a stop he leaped from the cab and was the first to reach the dead [girl]. He picked up the poor little crushed corpse in his arms and carried it into a cottage beside the road. A woman brought a light to see if she knew who it was that the train had killed. Denis tried not to look, but something impelled him to bend over the face of the dead, and he staggered back, shaking as one with the palsy. The dead girl was the girl he had seen at the looms in the cotton mill window. The woman told him it was Josephine Ladue.

Mahoney didn't take the flyer through Lakeside the next night, but the man who did took back to Denis a story that made him quake.

"The girl you killed last night," he told Denis, "was in the mill window when we came through. I saw her and others saw her and the mill watchmen, they say, swears she was at the looms at midnight. When we struck the crossing where you hit her the headlight went out. I don't like it, Denis."

Mahoney didn't take the flyer out for nearly a month, and when he did the tales that came to him of the headlight being extinguished every night at the crossing where he killed Josephine Ladue and of her being seen in the mill and by trainmen as they went by the Queen City took the sand out of him – the little that was left.

The first night back Mahoney's headlight was blown out at the crossing and he saw the smiling face of Josephine Ladue at the mill window, just as he had seen it on the night the flyer killed her. At the end of the run, he spoke of it as "a fancy," but nevertheless he ordered a new headlight, which was the third that had been put on the flyer since the Lakeside killing. Other engineers had found fault with it, too.

But the next night the new headlight failed at the Lakeside crossing and Denis Mahoney saw Josephine Ladue in the mill window. He called the girl's face "a fancy" and cussed the headlight. The "Fancy" was in the window every night, however, when he went by, and one day he laid off his run and went to Lakeside. It was the day he met William Dugan, the old watchman of the Queen City Mill. Dugan had resigned. He told Mahoney that it was because he couldn't stand seeing Josephine Ladue at the looms at night when he knew that she was dead and buried.

A few weeks ago, Denis Mahoney "got his," as his kind says, "in a head-on collision only a few hundred feet from the spot where Josephine Ladue was killed by the Burlington Flyer and where his "fancy" sat in a mill window. He went out, just as he had expected for a year that he would go -quick and violently. He had prayed against it, but it was of no use.

Since Mahoney's death an appeal has been made to the state board of railroad commissioners to change the grade crossing of the Rutland railroad. Those with whom the petition originated live near the railroad tracks and some of them accept the ghost as a matter of faith and others profess to have seen it, but whatever the motives of the petitioners as a whole may be, they are known as "the Lakeside ghost layers."

Thanks to Chris Woodyard and Ken Summers.

SOURCES:

- *Biennial Report of the Railroad Commissioner of the State of Vermont for 1899-1900 ["June 29, 1900. – Masie Blair, aged 22 years, while attempting to cross the tracks of the Rutland Railroad at Burlington, ahead of an approaching train, was struck by the engine and instantly killed."]*

- *Burlington [VT] Free Press: Dec. 4, 1900; June 30, 1900; May 8, 1901; Nov 12, 1901; Nov 21, 1901: Oct 31, 1999*

- *Repository [Canton, OH] 24 December 1905: p. 15*

- *"The Cotton Mill Ghost" by Joseph A. Citro from Weird Hauntings, Joanne Austin Ed. Sterling. NY 2006*

- *Historic Guide to Burlington Neighborhoods, David J. Blow et.al. CCHS, 1990*

The DUTTON House

"People have had experiences here. There are several guides that will not work here. Some staff are concerned about things they've seen or heard here."

– *Dan Cole, Supervisor of Museum Security*

The Dutton House

I can't recall much of anything my father was afraid of, and I don't remember ever seeing him frightened. But he was a storyteller, so sometimes he talked about being scared. In fact, when I was a kid, he told me about the two instances when he was almost terrified.

The first was while he was making his way across a narrow railroad trestle in Ludlow, Vermont. It was a bleak, tempestuous night with howling winds and a punishing torrent of rain. A train bore down on him, but he didn't realize it; the storm had muted its clatter and roar. When he finally heard the muffled whistle and saw the hazy light moving toward him, he realized the trestle was too long; he'd never be able to get off in time.

The only reason this story has a happy ending is that my father happened to light a cigarette just before he heard the train. The engineer somehow saw the flare of the match through the rain and hit the brakes, slowing down just enough so my father could escape in one piece. A good story I suppose, but I generally don't repeat it because it casts smoking in too favorable a light. It also raises a few other questions that I prefer not to examine too closely.

The important thing is that my father survived and lived to tell me about his second big scare: the Dutton house.

Years ago, for reasons I cannot remember, he and I were in Cavendish, standing across the street from an empty lot.

"Used to be a haunted house over there," he said matter-of-factly.

Instantly, I was all ears. I looked at the vacant space with elevated interest, trying to imagine what the building might have looked like. I pictured a night-black, castle-like affair with lightning bolts flashing in the background and bats swooping, sailing, and perching like miniature gargoyles.

The story my father told was nothing like that.

The Dutton House began life as a typical colonial saltbox, constructed there in 1782. Its builder, Salmon Dutton, was one of those energetic, multitalented men who prospered in small Vermont towns in the years following the Revolutionary War. The house was first used as his family residence and office. There Mr. Dutton conducted his surveying business. Additionally, he owned a toll road, was a justice of the peace, and treasurer for the town of Cavendish.

Salmon's descendants continued to own the place and occupied it until 1900. Over the years multiple modifications and additions continually accommodated the family's various business ventures. The place was used as a store, an inn, a tavern, and a boarding house for local mill workers. Over the years the old walls witnessed a lot of comings and goings, conventional and presumably criminal.

But when the Duttons abandoned the place at the turn of the twentieth century, it sat there boarded-up and deserted for a full fifty years.

Inevitably the dark, scary-looking place picked up the reputation of being haunted. Everyone around knew to avoid it; after all, there were ghosts inside, and God knows what else! Weird noises emanated from within. At night people saw dim lantern light moving behind dusty windowpanes. Perhaps Salmon Dutton himself walked the empty rooms and collapsing stairways. Or perhaps it was his wife, Sarah, a family member, or one of the many people who stayed, or died, in the ancient rooms when the place had been an inn.

Salmon Dutton's derelict saltbox was a breeding ground for scary stories, and I'm certain my father knew every one of them.

But he was involved in only one.

In the mid-1930s, hyped-up by fright, curiosity, and boyish bravado, he and two of his friends ventured there. To make it a good story, let's say it was around Hallowe'en, but I don't remember for sure. Anyway, while my father and another boy stood in front, trying to peer in through the slats of the boarded windows, the third friend went around back to search for a way to get inside.

Suddenly my father heard a terrified cry. The third boy bolted from behind the house and dashed across the street. From the safety of the far side – roughly where my father and I were standing when he first told me the story – the boy cried for the others to hurry. "We gotta get out of here!" he said over and over, "Come on! We gotta go. Now!" His face was wild, his eyes glassy with tears.

And they tore away. No one dared to look back.

Never again did they visit the Dutton House.

In all the years between then and 1970 when my father died, his friend would never reveal what he had seen that had frightened him so much.

But back to the house itself.

In the late 1940s, Salmon Dutton's great-great-grandson gave the house to the Vermont Historical Society. A historic treasure to be sure, but an expensive one to restore and maintain. The expected improvements never came.

Locals saw their haunted house as an eyesore that should be torn down so the road could be widened or new businesses put up.

As the shadow of the wrecking ball got closer, suspense built for those who cared about the welfare of the historic place.

Its salvation came in the form of a new museum that had recently opened 90 miles to the north: The Shelburne Museum, whose mission was "to show the craftsmanship and ingenuity of our forebears." They took over ownership of the Dutton House and performed a sort of miracle.

In 1950 they took the whole place apart, board by board, and moved it the 90 miles to Shelburne. There it was reassembled on the museum grounds. It was their first acquisition, and it is on exhibit to this day.

But here's the weird thing: The Dutton House ghost seems to have moved with it. An ever-lengthening list of seemingly inexplicable occurrences suggests that the Shelburne Museum is the only museum in the country that exhibits a real haunted house.

(Here I should probably add that it is not displayed as a haunted house, but rather as a traditional colonial saltbox. The term "saltbox" refers to the asymmetrical roof line said to resemble the profile of an early wooden container for salt.)

I first learned of the relocated ghost from a retired woman who volunteered as a guide at the museum. "They don't much like us to talk about it," she told me. "But anyone working in the house knows about it. Even some of the visitors have had experiences...."

"Experiences?" I wanted to know more.

So I tracked down one of the museum security guards, Mr. Burt Levitt, who routinely patrolled the house. His habit was to first check the whole building to be sure no one was hiding anywhere. But he told me, before he'd leave and lock-up, he'd always stop by the front door and listen. Often, he'd hear footsteps walking around upstairs. Footsteps in a room he knew to be empty.

So, just to be sure, he'd go back up to double check. The result was always the same: nothing.

However, when I visited the house on museum grounds, I saw something upstairs that would bring a slight chill to even the warmest heart. On exhibit around the fireplace, you'll find a number of adult-size cradles that long ago were used to comfort the old folk by rocking them near the fire. They are the size and shape of coffins. I can't help but see them as sort of a last resting place between this world and the next.

And, while making his midnight rounds, Mr. Levitt would often discover them in the dark empty room, rocking... back and forth... all by themselves. Those oversized cradles creaked and swayed, just as if their invisible occupants slumbered there.

His colleagues reported odd experiences of their own. Some heard kids' laughter in the upstairs rooms. Others heard a little girl crying. One guard was shaken at the sight of an unearthly face hovering outside a second-story window, peering in at him.

With slamming doors and other unidentifiable noises resounding overhead, it didn't take employees long to realize that the ghost – whoever it may be – seems to favor the upstairs. There some people have seen flashing lights; some felt cold breezes blowing through the rooms on hot summer nights. Needless to say, no air conditioning had been installed in this 1782 saltbox. There is nothing to disturb the air, much less account for the breezes.

Apparently one of the spectral residents will occasionally take a rest. On certain mornings museum staff will discover a specific upstairs bed dramatically disturbed. Sometimes bedclothes display a human-like impression, clearly visible. At other times sheets and blankets are found in wild disarray. Admittedly there could be more earthly explanations for such a phenomena, but so far there have been no confessions.

On the high end of the weirdness scale, full-form phantoms – real ghosts – have been witnessed in the Dutton House. No one has ever been able to identify any of the apparitions, but their variety does reinforce the idea that the place houses more than one ethereal tenant.

In 2005 two security guards (these days they travel in pairs) heard feet pounding overhead. One guard remained by the door as the other raced upstairs, certain he was about to trap an intruder.

He was shocked to find a terrified little girl standing at the foot of one of the beds. He turned away to call his partner, then looked back. In that head-turning instant the girl had vanished, leaving only an empty bed and a grandly perplexed guard, standing all alone in the spooky upstairs bedroom.

One elderly tour guide, the pseudonymous "Gladys Whipple," was working alone in the room directly above the tavern. Though she hadn't heard anyone come up the stairs, nor seen anyone enter the room, she suddenly felt as if she were not alone. Holding her breath, she furtively glanced around. There, standing in a corner and just watching her, she saw an unsavory looking stranger. Something was very wrong with what she saw; it just didn't make sense: The antiquated clothing. The malicious scowl.

When their eyes met, the specter actually growled at her. As Gladys hurried down the stairs, the apparition followed. Then it pursued her through the door and into the yard. One moment it was there, the next it was gone.

Not surprisingly, Gladys says she'll never enter the Dutton House again.

Many museum employees feel the same way.

Not long ago I joined Erin Conners at the Dutton House where we filmed a Hallowe'en segment for WPTZ Channel 5. We talked with Katie Krieger, who'd had a horrible experience her very first day on the job.

She hadn't had time to hear any of the ghost stories, but while she looked through the attic of the Dutton House, she heard something that sounded like a growl. There, in a dark corner of the attic, huddled under the eaves, she saw the crouching figure of a man. His white shirt first caught her eye, then she quickly realized the scruffy-looking fellow wore antique clothing.

The apparition disturbed her so much that she left hurriedly and refused to go back inside.

With great difficulty – and with a whole TV crew for backup– we coaxed her to go back in for another peek. It was broad daylight, but the poor young woman never stopped shaking. Her fear was genuine, obviously based on what for her had been a real and terrifying experience.

Back in Cavendish, the lot where the Dutton House once stood is no longer vacant. It has been converted into a pleasant little public park containing a highly detailed memorial plaque to one of America's oddest celebrities: Phineas Gage. Mr. Gage was a local railroad man who suffered a horrible accident. A 13-pound iron rod was blown into his skull, through his brain, and out the top of his head. Not only did he survive, he never even lost consciousness.

My father told me about him, too.

But that is another story....

T GRISWOLD
h MURDER
e House

"We have to record this morning a murder in our neighboring town of Williston, the shocking details of which we are not able to give in full, but the information we have thus far obtained, show it to have been of a most horrid character."

– Burlington (Vt.) Times, Aug. 29, 1865

The Griswold Murder House

The town history calls it "The Griswold Murder House," but it could as easily be called "Williston's ¬House of Horror."

According to local legend – together with owner testimony – the place is haunted. Over the years various occupants have reported many ghostly deeds: rumpled beds in which nobody slept, unseen companions, accurate warnings of disaster, and more. Though these benign indications of a haunting may seem unremarkable, this particular case illustrates an odd phenomenon: the backstory is – at least to me – far more terrifying than the ghost tale.

Before their stately federal style brick house existed, Sally and Ephraim Griswold were struggling farmers living on the edge of poverty. Then news of the California Gold strike hit Vermont. In 1850 the couple packed up and headed west to seek their fortune.

Ephraim quickly grew discouraged and returned to Vermont. But his wife, the indomitable Sally, stayed on.

Although she may have continued prospecting on the side, she saw there was bigger money to be made in easier, more dependable ways. The rapidly swelling population of the Sacramento area caused rents and real estate prices to skyrocket.

Never lacking vision, Sally opened a high-priced tavern and boarding house where she was able to get exorbitant prices for everything: for example, she sold eggs for as much as $10 apiece. That would be about $300 in 2016's money.

To protect herself against the undesirable and criminal aspects of the area – she apparently didn't consider herself among them – Sally enlisted with Sacramento Vigilantes, a tough group of almost-legal enforcers.

The point is Sally Griswold was smart and knew how to protect herself.

By the time she returned home to Vermont, she had amassed a fortune. It was hers and hers alone.

After reconnecting with Ephraim, Sally began to boast to her Williston neighbors that she was about to build the finest house in town.

Always true to her word, the construction was quickly accomplished; the place was ready by 1852, complete with a ballroom, crystal chandeliers, and views of distant Lake Champlain.

Sally, now in her fifties, was described as about five feet tall, weighing 130 pounds, and in excellent health. She was exceedingly active for her years. Often neighbors saw her at work in the fields, mowing, hoeing, plowing, and so forth.

Childless till this point, she and Ephraim suddenly had a family when they took in Adelia, the daughter of Sally's sister.

But in spite of all the home-town success and apparent normalcy, eccentric elements of Sally's character began to show, soon becoming more evident.

She was known to have lost interest in her husband, worked the farm mostly by herself, bossed everything and everyone, and slept alone in a seven by eight-foot spare room off the kitchen, choosing it over any of the home's formal, far more comfortable bedrooms.

When Adelia reached adulthood, she took up with a local lad named Charles Potter. We know that initially he must have passed muster with Sally and Ephraim because in 1862 the youngsters were allowed to be married. After that, they too moved into the Griswold house.

There all four lived in perfect disharmony. As an old account says, "Mrs. Griswold would sometimes quarrel with people: she was easily excited and was apt to get out of humor." In modern parlance, she became more cranky, disagreeable, and impossible to get along with. In fact, there were many people in the area who disliked her immensely. Her son-in-law, Charles, became such a person. Though eccentric and ornery, she was nonetheless perceived as wealthy, respectable, and a solid member of the Williston community.

While her husband, Ephraim, remained essentially a nonentity, Sally and her new son-in-law were like oil and water. As Sally became more crotchety, Charles Potter became more assertive. It was clear he wanted to run the farm and, perhaps, control the purse strings. The old woman and the young man would quarrel and butt heads almost every day, about almost anything. That they never came to blows is not a historical certainty.

Charles knew his wife would eventually inherit when Sally passed on. And he, like everyone in Williston, suspected the old woman was hiding a considerable treasure trove of valuables – possibly California gold – somewhere in the house or on the property.

During one evening meal, with guests at the table, Sally pitched one of her fits and stomped out of the room. Charles Potter was heard to mutter, "God may have His devil, but none so great as the one I have." He then said, more quietly, "I will give $200 to get that old devil out of the way; yes, by God, I'll give $500!"

One night not long afterward, while Charles, Adelia, and Ephraim were on a trip to Canada, Sally was left alone in the house with a twelve-year-old hired boy named Edward Call.

That night, August 28, 1865, something terrible happened.

The next morning Morris Sullivan arrived at the Griswold house to return a borrowed wagon. It was eight o'clock. The place was strangely still. Sally was always an early riser and normally would be up and about, working or scolding or feeding the chickens.

Puzzled, Mr. Sullivan stood still, undecided what to do. And then, "Help me; I'm locked in. Help!" It was the voice of the youngster, Eddie Call.

Mr. Sullivan went in to assist and found the lad had been imprisoned in his room. A stick was jammed in over the latch, making it impossible to open.

Upon release the boy seemed fine, but where was Mrs. Griswold? Spotting traces of what looked like blood on the doorstep, Mr. Sullivan became alarmed. He sent Eddie off to summon help while he explored the house. Neighbors quickly joined him, proceeding nervously with a tour of the premises.

When they opened the kitchen door, they discovered a pool of blood near the stove, and other marks of violence. Doors to the dining-room, the sitting-room, and a private room where Mrs. Griswold kept her jewelry, had all been forced open, apparently with a chisel. Upper drawers of the bureau containing valuables were broken open and rifled.

They discovered more blood smears on the windowsills in the dining and sitting rooms.

Mrs. Griswold's tiny sleeping room was empty. It was immediately obvious that the bedclothes were missing. Blood streaked the floor. But Mrs. Griswold was nowhere in the house.

Next, they made a diligent search of the outbuildings. When they reached the calf pen their quest was over.

What they found there was appalling: the corpse of Sally Griswold, the lower portion entirely exposed, the upper covered with a blanket and bed quilt.

As reported in the August 29, 1865, edition of the Burlington (Vt.) Times: "They found wounds on the left side of the head, fracturing the skull, which were undoubtedly produced by some blunt instrument. On the right side of the head were four or five contusions, probably made by the same instrument. There were also several stabs in the neck, one about two inches in length, from left to right, and severing the right external jugular vein. These wounds were evidently made by some sharp pointed instrument. Two cuts were found on the back of the left hand, also on the back of the right hand, and one an inch and a half deep on the left side of the chin, passing to the right up to the center of the lip. The knees were badly bruised, as was the left side of the chest. These wounds all tended to show that the murdered woman must have had a violent struggle for her life."

Murder most foul. There could be no doubt. Immediately three suspects leapt to mind:

(1.) Ephraim Griswold, husband, who over the years, had suffered myriad marital indignities and had no control over the land nor the money... while Sally was alive.

(2.) Adelia Potter, adopted daughter, who, according to Sally's will, was to inherit everything.

(3.) Charles Potter, son-in-law, who had made public his dislike for Sally, had apparently wanted her dead, and who claimed inside information that the old woman was about to change her will, cutting out Adelia and Charles altogether.

The only problem: these three prime suspects were known to be not only out of town, but also out of the country, at the time of the crime.

So, suspicion could fall on... anyone. Most townspeople knew about, and perhaps coveted, Sally's hidden fortune in California gold. And clearly the murderer, or murderers, had been looking for it.

L. B. Englesby, the State's Attorney, decided to bring in the heavy weaponry. He enlisted the services of a private detective from Burlington, former sheriff and renowned investigator, Noble Flanagan.

Mr. Flanagan was tireless and thorough. He began his very first day on the job at the crack of dawn, then labored well into the night.

After only a couple of days of snooping and questioning, Mr. Flanagan reported, "I asked practically everybody over at Williston if they'd seen any strangers around recently. Well, several of them had apparently seen the same person and in every case, he was either inquiring about Charles Potter or was in Potter's company."

Mr. Flanagan had also learned some important local scuttlebutt: townsfolk believed that Mrs. Griswold's entire estate – at least $50,000 plus any hidden fortune – was to go to her adopted daughter Adelia, and therefore to her husband Charles Potter. However, recently Mrs. Griswold had threatened to change her will because of her growing dissatisfaction with her son-in-law.

Motive for sure. But with the trio of primary suspects in Canada at the time of the murder, the stranger, Mr. Flanagan reasoned, must have been an accomplice. Maybe even a hired killer.

Mr. Flanagan's reputation as a sleuth was well earned and perfectly demonstrated in the Griswold Case. He soon identified the stranger as John Ward, alias Jerome Levigne. He traced Mr. Ward to New York City whence he had come to Williston to do his unholy business.

Detective Flanagan tracked John Ward down in New York City only to discover that he was about to depart for Vermont again, either to collect his pay or possibly to commence a blackmail scheme against Mr. Potter.

Detective Flanagan boarded the train back to Vermont and kept an eye on the thug all the way. Later, at the trial, he stated, "As the [train] cars stopped, the prisoner attempted to step off as usual. I then reached down, seized him by the collar, hauled him up on the platform, and told him that I must make a prisoner of him. He asked what was the accusation. I replied, 'Nothing but murder.' He said, 'That is very strange, as he was an entire stranger and was never through here before in the world.'"

Mr. Flanagan also testified, "I commenced searching him; the first thing I took out of his hand was a 'seven-shooter,' loaded. I next drew out of his waist band a 'spring billy' [or as we call it today, a collapsible baton]. I also found on him a lancet and a bottle of chloroform, found in his coat pocket, among a parcel of songs, a certain paper...."

A paper incriminating Charles Potter.

After that, evidence against John Ward, AKA Jerome Levigne,

continued to mount.

He and Charles Potter were brought to trial. It was one of Vermont's most exciting, covered in newspapers all around the country.

The outcome:

John Ward, alias Jerome Levigne, was found guilty of murder and was sentenced to be hanged by the neck until dead. He was shipped off to the Vermont State Prison in Windsor where he was kept in solitary confinement for one year. Then he was brought out and executed. He was 27 years old.

Charles Potter, though acquitted of the Sally Griswold murder, continued making trips to Canada. After a while it became clear that he was involved in smuggling and counterfeiting. He and Adelia remained married and partners in crime. In July of 1868 they were caught in the act of robbing Smith Wright's store in Williston. Adelia was apprehended while exiting via a rear window. Later, in jail, during a disagreement with another female inmate, she was smashed over the head with a flatiron. Adelia died as a result. It was 1872. She was 42 years old.

Charles followed her to the grave ten years later. He had gotten away with murder and countless other crimes and misdemeanors.

Today Charles and Adelia are still together, buried side-by-side in the Eldredge Cemetery in South Burlington.

Ephraim – who may or may not have knowingly participated in his wife's death – died in 1886. He was never arrested nor seriously considered as a murder suspect.

And then, of course, there is our heroine: Sally Griswold herself.

Though today her body lies in a Williston cemetery, her spirit could still be with us. The family who purchased the house in the 1980s claims Sally might well be on the premises. To them her presence is benign, somewhat comforting, and protective. They refer to her as "Aunt Sally."

The room that had been Sally Griswold's bedroom is almost never used.

It has become something of a showroom, full of antiques. A vintage spread covers a bed that is rarely occupied. Nonetheless, the present owner has repeatedly entered the room to find the bedspread disheveled or, perhaps more strangely, left with an indentation, as if someone had been sitting on it. Her husband, the only other person in residence, would unfailingly deny culpability. The owner would straighten the spread and shut the door, only to find the bed disorganized the next time she went in.

She has come to believe that Aunt Sally is very much a part of the household, guarding against further intruders and disasters.

For example, she recalls the day she drove into the village on an errand. Oddly, the farther down the road she traveled the more she experienced an inexplicable and urgent compulsion to return to the house. Finally, she turned the car around and went back, feeling somewhat sheepish for giving in to such an odd impulse. As she opened the back door, she saw smoke pouring out of the basement. The furnace lining had collapsed. Had she delayed but a few minutes more, the house would have burned down!

If Sally is still there, she is living in harmony with the new stewards of the property. Nowadays there is none of the discord she had endured back in the time of Ephraim, Adelia, and Charles Potter.

Perhaps Sally's first appearance as a "ghost" occurred at a distant location under very unusual circumstances.

Cut to Chittenden, Vermont.

It is a matter of history that in the 1870s William and Horatio Eddy conducted elaborate materialization séances upstairs in their farmhouse. Every night, night after night (with the exception of Sundays), dozens of apparitions would appear on an elevated platform. The specters were so vivid and stunning that spectators came from all over the world to witness them. Thanks to the Eddy brothers, Vermont became known as "The Spirit Capital of the Universe." It was the place "to be," if you were a spirit.

In 1874 the Eddys' vexing spiritualistic phenomena were

investigated by Col. Henry Steel Olcott, a detective and reporter from New York City. Col. Olcott arrived a skeptic and, nine weeks later, left a believer.

In his book *People of the Other World*, Col. Olcott carefully documented the various spirits that he encountered, including one he called "The Murdered Woman." That "Woman" was apparently Sally Griswold. He wrote, "After her murder the woman appeared there [at the Eddy house] with all her wounds upon her and described the whole scene..." including the motive. The apparition was recognized by people who had known Mrs. Griswold in life.

Col. Olcott's idea was a daring one. In the concluding chapter of his book he wrote: "If materialized spirits can address audiences, as I have heard them in the Eddy house, is there any reason why, after a time, they may not take the stand in a court of justice and testify against their murderers?" They could, "stalk into the presence of judge and jury and show their bleeding wounds to the horror-stricken assassin."

Col. Olcott saw a future application of Spiritualism as a tool for justice more certain than a lie detector.

Of course, this "Spectral Evidence" never became part of the American Judicial System. It was the legwork of the indefatigable Noble Flanagan that brought Sally Griswold's murderer to justice. And who knows, maybe John Ward, alias Jerome Lavigne, is getting his earthly punishment extended in the "Other World."

And I am left wondering if Mr. and Mrs. Potter are getting their just deserts in the other world as well, since they escaped proper punishment in this one.

ADDITIONAL INFORMATION:

As an addendum to this chapter – and for the serious history buffs among us – here is what Col. Olcott wrote in his book *People of the Other World*, in a section called "Future Uses of Spiritualism" (page 417).

[I] content myself with recording the fact that the phenomena of Chittenden are apparently real, at least to a certain extent, and they cannot be ignored any longer.

And now let me state a few facts by way of conclusion.

I have heretofore confined my narrative to accounts of the reunion of separated families and the visits of friendship made by the people of the other world to those they love in this. I have reserved for my last chapter an incident that shows that the time has possibly come when the trite adage "murder will out" is to have a terrible significance. It is always so much pleasanter to dwell upon the agreeable than the horrible, upon what attracts and charms rather than upon that which startles and appalls, that, I take it, no further explanation will be required of the fact above stated. But if any other reason were needed for the reservation of the story of the Griswold murder for the last chapter, it may be found in my desire to leave upon the minds of a certain class of readers a strong impression that, should the investigation of these spiritual phenomena result in the confirmation of their verity, a most important source of aid to the cause of justice might thus be discovered and availed of.

If materialized spirits can address audiences, as I have heard them in the Eddy house, is there any reason why, after a time, they may not take the stand in a court of justice and testify against their murderers? What a day to be remembered would that be when the fictions of Shakespeare's imagination should be paralleled by the facts coming within our personal experience; when our modern Hamlets, Banquos, and Duncans would stalk into the presence of judge and jury and show their bleeding wounds to the horror-stricken assassin.

Now, of course, this will appear absurd to the great majority of persons who read this, and so it would have seemed to me before I went to Chittenden and saw what I did there; but what does the reader say when I tell him that on the evening of September 28th I saw the spirit of a woman who was murdered on the night of Sunday, August 27th, 1865, at Williston, Vt., by a New York rough named John Ward alias Jerome Lavigne, by the procurement of her son-in-law, Charles Potter? That after her murder the woman appeared there with all her wounds upon her and described the whole scene? Does that look as if it were quite so absurd to imagine that the same thing may, one day, be seen in a courtroom, either with or without the presence of a "materializing medium?" It is prophesied by the spirits at Eddys' that next September they will address the audience in that circle-room in full light and with people sitting about them upon the platform; why should not an equal effort be made to deter from crime, and, if need be, punish it?

Mrs. Sarah Walker Griswold, a lady sixty years of age, lived with her husband on their farm in the town of Williston, and their adopted daughter and niece and her husband, Charles Potter. On the morning of the murder, the Potters, their children, old Mr. Griswold, and Potter's brother went to Canada, leaving with Mrs. Griswold only a small boy, about thirteen years of age. On Monday morning a neighbor went to the house and discovered the body of Mrs. Griswold lying, half-naked, in a calf-pen some rods from the house, in a horribly mutilated condition.

The surgeons "found wounds on the left side of the head, fracturing the skull, which were undoubtedly produced by some blunt instrument. On the right side of the head were four or five contusions, probably made by the same instrument. There were also several stabs in the neck, one about two inches in length, from left to right, and severing the right external jugular vein. These wounds were evidently made by some sharp-pointed instrument. Two cuts were found on the back of the left hand, also on the back of the right hand, and one an inch and a half deep on the left side of the chin, passing to the right up to the centre of the lip. The knees were badly bruised as was the left side of the chest."

In due course of time the murderer was tracked and brought to justice; and the guilt of Potter being brought home to him, he also fell into the hands of the law. The artist has represented, in the picture accompanying this, the appearance of the spirit of Mrs. Griswold when she first came to the Eddy circle-room. When I saw her, she presented a natural appearance, and was neatly attired in a white dress. On a previous occasion she was seen by a friend who knew her in life, a Mr. P. P. Wilkins, of Winooski Falls (Vt.), who writes me that: "Mrs. Griswold materialized herself and I recognized her. She grasped my hand and presented me with a flower." The motive prompting Potter to the murder was a threat on her part to change her will so as to cut off his wife and himself from any share in her property, which she had accumulated in California in the course of a long residence there.

Thanks to Mark Hutchins, Jim Heltz, and Arnold Wetherhead.

ST. ALBANS

Mr. Raymond Shepard of St. Albans was 93 years old. Yet he had vivid recall of an incident he experienced when he was a boy of ten. Nothing remotely like it ever happened in the subsequent eight decades of his life. As he told me in a July, 1998 interview,

"People don't believe in ghost stories, but this is what actually happened."

Back in **1915** his family lived in a large house on Aldis Street. It was next to the last house on the right, not far from the railroad yard where his father worked as a fireman.

Once or twice a week his parents would go to the silent movies at the Empire Theater in town.

Mr. Shepard and his brother Harold would stay home to keep an eye on the baby.

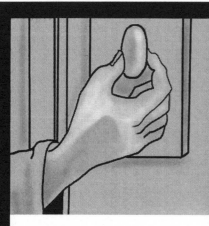

Harold was three years older, so he was in charge. After the parents left, Harold locked the front door behind them.

Then he ran upstairs to check on the baby, who was sleeping comfortably in his crib.

"This particular night", Mr. Shepard told me, "Harold and I were sitting around in the dining room, which was just one side of the parlor. And we sat there and played these old cylindrical — type records".

"And just as I was changing a record I heard some footsteps. I didn't pay too much attention to it."

"I did get up to look through the parlor to see if it was the baby walking downstairs. There was nothing."

"So I went back and changed the record, then we went and popped some popcorn. And we sat there eating popcorn and listening to the music." After the song ended the boys heard the same sound again. Louder. More distinct. It was unmistakable this time. Someone was coming down the stairs.

Raymond said to Harold, "I bet the little bugger's got out of his crib and he's coming downstairs!"

So he got up and waited behind the heavy drapes that separated the parlor from the front hall. "The curtain was closed," Mr. Shepard said. "I wanted to surprise him, let him know I knew he was coming."

We heard him walking. The stairs were creaking. The sound got down to where I figured he was about to the bottom. I pulled the drapes open, quick like that, and said, ' What are you trying to do, surprise us?' And there was nobody there." It seemed impossible. And scary. With that, both boys began to worry.

"We finally got our courage together to go up and see if the baby had got out of the crib. So the both of us went upstairs. We were more or less scared by then. And we went into the bedroom and the baby was sound asleep. Never had been out of the crib at all".

At that point their fear escalated. "We swore somebody had been walking down the stairs. We both started crying, hoping the folks would come home".

By the time their parents got home they were too frightened to unlock the front door. "We were scared to go past the bottom of the stairs in the hallway."

Raymond and Harold told their parents why they were so frightened, and the whole matter was put to rest. For a while.

Sometime later the family was entertaining guests in the living room. Another brother, Henry, was positioned in such a way that he could see into the kitchen beyond. All of a sudden movement caught his eye.

Mr. Shepard recalled, "He looked and when he did he saw a sleeve – of a nightgown or a dress – in the door. . . waving. He got up and walked towards it. As he got close, it disappeared".

Puzzled, Henry walked into the kitchen and looked around, trying to figure where the thing had gone.

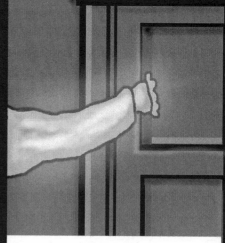

In a moment he saw it again. It had reappeared in the hallway. He saw it in front of the doorway leading to the basement.

But when Henry got to the cellar door, the sleeve had vanished again. The bewildered boy searched the cellar, but could find nothing that might account for the odd vision.

When he told the people about it, they were equally mystified. But, Raymond Shepard said, "We got our proof from the neighbor lady who lived next door."

During a chance conversation with their next-door neighbor, Henry described the sleeve and the odd ruffles he unmistakably observed.

The lady seemed to go white as he spoke. Finally, with wonder in her voice, she said, "That's just the gown that I put on the baby when it died. What you describe is identical to the gown we put on the baby."

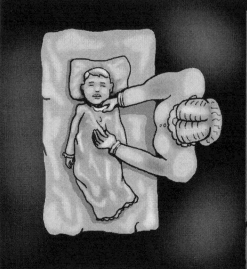

She went on to explain how the people who had lived in the house before the Shepards had had a baby who died there. The lady had personally dressed the baby for burial. She recalled the gown she had used.

One can imagine the chill the Shepard family felt when they got the news. But the real kicker came some years later, after the Shepards had moved to another St. Albans home.

News got out that the occupant of the house had found something gruesome in the cellar. There, buried in the earthen floor, they discovered the body of a baby, the baby the neighbor had dressed for burial. Unbeknownst to her, they had buried the child in the cellar.

Mr. Shepard recalled "They dug up the box and reburied it". This time properly, in the cemetery.

Raymond Shepard had a long and productive life. He married a local girl and they raised a family. He worked forty-one years in the oil delivery business. Had a second career at General Electric in Burlington. Then generated retirement income as an elementary school bus driver.

But never, in all that time, did he experience anything to compare with the odd occurrences in his own house.

"That's the God's honest truth," he said. "Somebody was trying to tell us the baby was in the cellar".

PART TWO

INTRODUCTION

In the first section of the book, I looked at what we conventionally think of as "ghosts," that is, people experiencing what they suspect of being the spirits of the dead.

The belief that the dead return is age-old and difficult to dislodge. It is nearly impossible to persuade people to discount the evidence of their own senses. "That was my dead mother. I saw her! How could I not recognize my own mother? I even smelled her Evening in Paris perfume!"

Like everyone else, I can't dismiss the evidence of my own senses, and what follows is a true story, accurate in every detail as best I can remember it. It is more autobiographical than I like to be, and slightly R-rated, so if you are uncomfortable with personal revelation or easily offended by references to the human body, you'd best skip this introduction and move forward to the next chapter.

The Night Visitor

In the early 1990s I had purchased a historic 1870s house in downtown Burlington (Vermont) where I was living alone while trying to maintain my writing career. This was not long after my mother had died, so I was perhaps not as psychologically comfortable as I would have liked.

I wasn't lonely. I had good friends and a special lady with whom I spent a fair amount of time. She taught at one of the nearby colleges, so we each went our own way professionally, but we got together whenever we could. Generally, weekends.

We'll call her Sheila.

On this particular weekend she had come to town to visit. We were sleeping in an enclosed upstairs porch overlooking Lake Champlain. Sometime during that dark night, I woke up and Sheila was not beside me. Now I *could* make her absence sound weird, but in reality, it wasn't.

A dim light visible through the slightly open door suggested she had gotten up to go to the bathroom.

Not a bad idea, I thought. I'll wait until she gets back, then I'll visit the bathroom, too.

I'm propped up on the pillows waiting for her to come back, realizing more and more how much I have to visit the toilet. Hurry up, I'm thinking.

Pretty soon she reenters the room and stands by the door, perfectly naked and smiling at me. So, putting Nature's urgings in their necessary sequence, I get out of bed and walk toward her on my way out the door. Everything seems perfectly normal as I pause, reaching out to touch her shoulder.

With that instant of what should have been hand-to-shoulder contact, there was a startling reality jolt - she just vaporized! I watched her instantaneously transform into a vaguely human-shaped blur. Then, like a special effect in a movie, she simply pixilated, and was gone!

Simultaneously, I heard the toilet flush and the real Sheila walked into the room.

"What's wrong with you?" she asked, apparently seeing me standing in the middle of the room with a muddled expression on my face.

"I... you..."

It didn't take me long to realize what had happened. There are certain psychological states during which we can be asleep and awake at the same time. During those moments when we are waking up, or drifting off to sleep, we can go through transitional levels of consciousness that psychologists refer to as hypnopompic or hypnagogic states. In fact, we are awake, and, at the same time, dreaming. Or, as in this case, hallucinating.

I was fast asleep but woke up enough to realize Sheila wasn't there. I consciously speculated that she was using the bathroom. Anticipating her return, I subconsciously created an accurate dream of her walking back into the room. Awake and asleep. Nothing weird or supernatural about it.

However, suppose my dream and hallucination had not been about Sheila. Suppose instead that it had been about my recently deceased mother. What if my dead mother had walked into my bedroom? I would have sworn – and would still be swearing – that I'd had a ghost experience. And my senses would have backed me up. "I was awake. I saw her. I even smelled her perfume!"

It is interesting to compare this experience with all the hundreds of anecdotes in books, newspapers, magazines, TV shows, and podcasts that begin with "I was in bed and...," or, "I was just waking up, and..."

Your senses, seemingly alert, tell you unambiguously that you are seeing something that is not there.

Ghosts are *something*.

What?

Spirits of the dead? I doubt it. Misperceptions? Often. Dreams or hallucinations? Sometimes. Exaggerations? Sure. Hoaxes? Yes, that can and does happen.

For the purposes of this book, it is not important what they are, or are not. It is only important that we admit that people do have "The Ghost Experience."

And to me it can include almost anything we have the urge to classify as "Supernatural": UFOs, curses, Bigfoots, gnomes, and on and on....

Never lose sight of the fact that the mind – or brain, if you prefer – has power. Mine was able to create a life-size replica of my friend Sheila. Are other minds capable of materializing something similar, but solid? A doppelganger? A tulpa?

The final two chapters of this book will look at "Vermont Ghost Experiences" of another nature... or supernature. These chapters are vastly separated in time, and, at least on the surface, seem very different. We will see that from the early days right up until now, there is magic in Vermont. I call it *The Vermont Ghost Experience*. You may decide to call it something else.

T JEWS of
h e MIDDLETOWN

*"We may have to fight dead men and devils
before we get fairly hold of it."*

– Daniel P. Thompson: May Martin, or The Money Diggers

The Jews of Middletown

Late 18th century Vermont was a weird time, a time of secrets, mystery, and magical happenings.

Among the era's mystical inclinations was a widespread fascination with treasure hunting. In a near-hysteria of belief, certain individuals ascribed to the notion that vast fortunes were buried underground, patiently waiting to be unearthed. The origins of this supposed occult wealth were diverse. Some thought pirates from Lake Champlain and the faraway seacoasts had ventured deeply inland to bury their ill-gotten gains. Others reckoned the fortunes had been stashed by some long-forgotten race who had inhabited the Green Mountains ages before the Abenaki. And of course, it was possible that more recent settlers, lacking banks and other trustworthy saving institutions, had buried their wealth for safekeeping, died, and left it there for later generations to discover.

But no matter where it came from, it was most assuredly there!

As you might expect, there was a supernatural element to all this speculation. Some folks thought malevolent spirits guarded the hidden loot. Others believed angelic entities would willingly assist seekers by pointing the way to the treasure trove. Discovery rituals were performed in darkest night, and in complete silence. Generally, one member of the excavation party would be assigned to read the Bible, hoping that would keep demonic forces at bay.

But in every case, some morally ambiguous – make that out and out "shady" – character would appoint himself to be the "keeper of the secrets." Only he could crack the code, interpret the symbols, translate the language, or read the map. Predictably, this energetic little genius would ultimately lead a band of gullible "investors" to the site of limitless wealth. Such a character drifted into Middletown, Vermont, about 1800. He called himself Mr. Winchell and he came equipped with a sharpened hazel rod that, he assured townsfolk, was a magical pointer stick capable of directing them to their buried fortunes.

Mr. Winchell's timing couldn't have been more precise.

As it turns out there was an equally sinister character already in town, perhaps waiting for Mr. Winchell's arrival. The meeting of the two would spark an alchemical overload, exploding into one of the strangest and most colorful episodes of Vermont history. Generally, it's referred to by the unfathomable title The Wood Scrape.

Middletown, Vermont – today's Middletown Springs – was settled before the Revolutionary War. Its Congregational Church was organized in 1782. Among the sparse population at that time lived an extraordinary character named Nathaniel Wood.

Apparently, Mr. Wood held strong religious beliefs which he spread using his charismatic charm and domineering personality. He claimed to have experienced some kind of religious awakening and was convinced he was a far more capable shepherd than the gentleman presiding in the Congregational pulpit.

It is no surprise that the church's governing body had an altogether different opinion. Mr. Wood's beliefs were so unorthodox, and Mr. Wood so overbearing, that they decided not only to reject him as their leader, but also to excommunicate him from the church.

But Nathaniel Wood was never one to take such rejection lightly. Rather than appeal the decision, he went off and set up his own church. And the "New Israelites" were born.

A bit about their belief system might give you some idea of why the New Israelites did not fit snugly into early rural Congregationalism.

Mr. Wood – or "Priest" Wood, as his followers began to call him – believed he and his disciples were the descendants of ancient Jews. They were therefore among God's chosen people, quite distinct from the lowly local "Gentiles" who made up the rest of the area's population.

In time Priest Wood's congregation grew while his claims became more grandiose. He said he had the power to cure all sorts of diseases, locate lost or stolen goods, even transform ordinary substances into precious metal.

Such gaudy assertions were bound to attract new followers of the credulous kind. Soon enrollment included the members of fifteen families. And more were eager to join. After all, who wouldn't want to be part of an exclusive group whose members were the descendants of the illustrious, Biblically celebrated, ancient Jews? Membership would guarantee newcomers surefire supernatural connections and heightened local influence.

Then Priest Wood's notions grew menacing.

He assured his followers that with divine assistance their cult would soon possess all the land for miles around. Why? Because nonmembers were going to be struck down. Wiped out. Erased! And there wasn't a blessed thing they could do to prevent it... except sign on with Priest Wood.

Sure enough, new fear brought new supporters.

It is at about this point that our old pal Mr. Winchell and his magical hazel rod enter the picture.

For a while after he arrived in town he had remained as a guest, or possibly a hired hand, at Ezekiel Perry's farm. There he was able to stay undetected for several months because the property was at the end of a long dirt road and seldom visited. He could also study the habits and inclinations of the local population.

Come spring, Mr. Winchell would make occasional fleeting appearances, always equipped with his Y-shaped stick. He'd have one end in each hand with the third pointing forward. It seemed to direct him in his wandering. Occasionally someone would ask him what he was doing.

"Oh, nothing at all," he would reply, "for the rod is doing all things itself."

The people thereabouts were not unfamiliar with "dowsing rods" and they recognized Mr. Winchell as what they called a "Water Witch" (a title presumably derived from "witch hazel" rather than witchcraft).

But Mr. Winchell, or his rod, claimed to be able to find more than water.

When the subject of finding treasure was cautiously introduced, Mr. Winchell said something like, "Why, pshaw, that's easily done!"

And he proceeded to prove it by allowing the rod to discover an ancient ox-shoe buried in the mud nearby. If it could detect ordinary metal, then, of course, it could detect precious metal.

Easy, indeed!

It wasn't long before Mr. Winchell had assembled a group of tight-lipped conspirators who were determined to put the "witch" and his rod to the test.

But before Mr. Winchell would agree to work with any of them, each man had to be tested. Were they sincere in their enterprise? Were they good and holy men? Would they keep the process a secret? Would they obey Mr. Winchell's every instruction?

Only the rod could answer. As it was passed before each man it dipped as if in affirmation.

Then the cluster of expectant townsfolk under "the sublime direction of the rod," followed Mr. Winchell to a hill somewhat east of Ezekiel Perry's house, not far from the Tinmouth line. There the rod began its gyrations. Mr. Winchell nodded sagely to let the group know that they had indeed found the location of their buried treasure.

Under his direction they labored for two or three days, using pickaxes and shovels to move away the tons of earth that separated them from endless fortune. If at length they began to seem discouraged, the rod would flex, and wriggle and Mr. Winchell would offer some new encouragement.

It was money, he said, silver and gold coins locked in an iron chest. They'd have it soon! All that remained to do was to move one large stone out of the way.

Soon, exactly as predicted, they unearthed a large flat stone. This should have come as no surprise because that rocky land is littered with them. Nonetheless, they were overjoyed. But Mr. Winchell became solemn and intense. "Don't touch it!" He cried with some urgency. Again, he consulted the rod and learned that they should wait a while before lifting the stone. Better, he said, to do it after dark. "People might be watching. Thieves might be ready to spring and steal it from us!"

Shocked silence! Stunned men looked around fearfully. Others glanced furtively at each other or stared at the ground.

"We must leave now," Mr. Winchell whispered, "and stay away until after sundown." Then, in the protection of shadows, they could come back with the tools they needed to do the job properly.

Disappointed, yet firm in their resolve, the men obediently went about their business, waiting for the sun to inch its way from the sky.

That night, burdened with heavy ropes, pickaxes, and prying bars, they reassembled.

Mr. Winchell addressed his eager crew, interpreting for them the instructions of the rod. "Soon we will uncover the chest, and each of us will be a wealthy man."

But there were some cautions and conditions.

First, he told them, you must remove any metal objects you may have on your person. Metal, he explained, may confuse and bewilder the rod.

Pocket knives, coins, nails, even belt buckles were neatly piled on the flat surface of a nearby stone.

Then, changing from affable to ominous, Mr. Winchell warned that there was some supernatural presence – he called it "a divinity" – guarding the hoard. If any among them didn't believe... if anyone lacked faith or failed to follow directions... And if anyone uttered so much as a word during the digging, that "divinity" would rush in, snatch away the money, and withhold it forever.

"And, my friends," Mr. Winchell cautioned portentously, "if that should happen, if we disturb or anger this intangible guardian, I cannot be held answerable for the consequences."

The men looked timidly at each other. Then nodded firm agreement.

In my mind's eye I see the dark scene very clearly. The moon is nearly full, its pale light casting jagged shadows of spindly trees across the site of the dig. With Mr. Winchell looking on, the men labor in near silence, making every effort to keep their shovels from scraping too loudly in the gravelly soil. No one speaks. Tightly crowded together, they pry, and lift, and push, and strain, and try not to get in each other's way – all the time maintaining an unnatural silence.

The stone seems way too large, impossible to coax from its bed in the earth.

Perhaps one of them became over-eager, perhaps someone lost his balance, or his foot slipped as he pressed his own weight against the immobile rock.

Whatever the cause, the effect shattered the silence: "Ahh! Damn it, man, you're tromping on my toes!"

And the spell was broken.

Mr. Winchell leapt up in a panic. More agitated than they had ever seen him, he cried, "The money is lost! Run, quickly. Run for your lives!"

The terrified crew scrambled away, as if the devil himself were snatching at their shirttails.

And Mr. Winchell plucked the coins from the pile of metal, where the men had left them for safekeeping.

One could spend a long time pondering whether it was chance or design that brought Mr. Winchell and Priest Wood to each other's attention. I think the meeting was inevitable. In small town Vermont, then as now, an anomaly like an animated rod would hit the gossip circuit and quickly reach all ears – especially those of the local religious zealot.

The big questions, of course, were these: Was Priest Wood taken in by Mr. Winchell? Or did Mr. Winchell convert and become a "New Israelite"? Or possibly the two were in league, planning the biggest scam in town history.

Then again, we must allow that there might truly have been a supernatural component thrown into this toxic mix.

Whatever the situation, a natural – or perhaps supernatural – partnership formed between the two men. The incredible "magic stick" could be seen a divine symbol, exactly the proof Priest Wood needed to corroborate his outlandish claims and to bring a rush of new converts to New Israel.

It appeared that Priest Wood apprenticed himself to the mysterious Mr. Winchell and began to learn the operation of what he now awarded the authoritative designation "St. John's Rod."

With the aid of this wonderful rod, all sorts of miracles seemed possible. Priest Wood began to feature it in his religious services. He – or any member of the congregation – could pose questions. The rod would tap and twitch in response. Priest Wood insisted that its jerking and flexing were heavenly answers to earthbound queries.

And just as expected, the antics of the magic stick brought many new converts. People saw St. John's Rod as tangible proof of a godly presence in their midst. It corroborated Priest Wood's link to divinity, and proved they, his growing following, truly were the chosen people.

For two years "The New Israelites" continued to use the rod

to find lost property, pass judgment on applicants, and to identify healing roots and herbs. And of course, the rod-directed money digging continued, bringing attention to the sect and coin to its coffers.

Their belief was unshakable: their benevolent deity would eventually lead them to an endless supply of riches. Thus, they could build their New Jerusalem and pave its streets with gold.

The rod was used to access any kind of information: it would predict the course of a person's illness up to and including death. It even instructed what medicine to administer.

St. John's Rod was used during public meetings, whether it was church or town business. Priest Wood issued the worrisome notion that it could "divine the thoughts and intentions of men."

It is likely that at the very beginning the greater population didn't pay much attention to the activities of the New Israelites, except maybe to chuckle at their antics. But as the claims became more grandiose and menacing, the sect could not be ignored. Remember, they claimed to be the descendants of the ancient Jews. This may have seemed an odd choice in an era when Jews were an unpopular lot. But nonetheless they had a reputation for being "mystical" and their place in the Bible gave them a certain stature that Priest Wood knew how to exploit.

Soon it became known that the New Israelites considered themselves the lawful owners of the whole country, which, of course, included the town of Middletown.

And, they said, God was going to step forward and prove it!

I suspect non-believers, if there were any at this point, were probably feeling a little nervous.

Reality shifted a bit more when the ambitious rod ordered the New Israelites to commence the construction of a temple – their very own house of worship.

Eagerly crews set to work. Everyone pitched in, preparing to be proud of their own exclusive temple, which would rival in grandeur and magnificence, the venerable cathedrals of Europe.

The timber was prepared, the frame raised as high as the rafters, everything was going along swimmingly until—

Another reality shift! The rod changed its mind. It ordered them to stop.

But why? What had gone wrong?

To find out, Priest Wood applied the rod in a unique manner; he used it as "a medium of revelation."

What he discovered sent a chill throughout the population. Something truly horrific was about to happen. The "New Israelites" stood aghast as the stick told them about a terrible earthquake that would soon lay waste to the entire world. It would be a new apocalypse. Near total destruction. Akin only to the great flood of Noah. In fact, it gave them a specific date: the night of January 14, 1802.

This time it was not to be a natural disaster (like floodwater), but supernatural, destruction wrought by the hand of Omnipotence. The earth would tremble, buildings topple, and mountains shatter. A "Destroying Angel" would come forth and wipe out all but the chosen.

Priest Wood stormed on about the ninth and eleventh chapters of Ezekiel, terrifying all he encountered. (And hadn't this all started when Mr. Winchell arrived in town at Ezekiel Perry's farm? Such coincidences can have portentous meaning!)

As the dreaded 14th of January approached, agitation increased among "Gentiles" throughout the town. They organized a militia that could mobilize at a moment's warning, in case they needed protection from the New Israelites, or God, or the floodwaters, or the "Destroying Angel," or whatever. In an effort to ensure no earthquakes were to be produced with man-made explosives, all the military stores – chiefly dynamite – were removed from the place where the town housed such things.

Meanwhile the New Israelites were abandoning their homes after posting messages on their doors that said, "Christ our Passover was sacrificed for us." This was to protect the house and valuables from natural, or supernatural, destruction.

By 9:00 the militia, headed by Captain Joel Miner, had posted armed guards at each of the four roads leading into town. A short time later six New Israelites appeared, making their way toward town. Some reports say they were in costume, that is, outfitted according to Ezekiel (ix, 2): "every man a slaughter weapon in his hand; and one man among them was clothed with linen, with a writer's inkhorn by his side...."

Well, maybe.

In any event, the guards saw this bizarre vision approaching and hailed them. When they didn't stop, the militiamen fired and the men fled.

About midnight, the same men approached the village from another direction. Again, they were hailed by the militiamen, again they were fired upon. When they dispersed a second time the strange drama – as opposed to the world – apparently ended.

Overall, the whole night was a bust for Priest Wood and his New Israelites. As with all end-of-the-world predictions – thus far, anyway – the fatal day came and went, and nothing happened. No earthquake, no smiting angels, no destruction of the Gentiles.

When the new day dawned, there was a lot of hemming and hawing among the faithful. These deluded souls, with "Christ our Passover" signs nailed to their doors, began to feel the "slow-moving finger of scorn" pointing at them.

Moreover, they feared the heavy hand of the law would soon descend upon them for their misdeeds. No doubt embarrassment turned to I-told-you-sos when the mysterious Mr. Winchell (aka Mr. Wingate), was identified as a wanted counterfeiter from Bradford, Vermont.

It wasn't long before Priest Wood and his family, the majority of their followers, and the contemptible Mr. Winchell, all disposed of their property and slunk off into the wilds of New York State, where, for a time, they disappeared.

One significant follow-up to the affair is its alleged relationship to Mormonism. Mr. Winchell and Oliver Cowdry (son of a prominent player in the Wood Scrape) subsequently moved to Palmyra, New York, where they became acquainted with another transplanted Vermonter, Joseph Smith, the founder of Mormonism. But, as historian David M. Ludlum cautions, "The strands of connection between the Wood Scrape and the Palmyra outcroppings are too tenuous to withstand historical criticism. Nevertheless, the two incidents suggest similar social tendencies in the soil of these two 'infected districts.'"

In many ways the Wood Scrape is typical of what was going on in Vermont at the time. People were looking for tangible manifestations to corroborate their religious beliefs, and a counterfeiting con man with a magic wand seemed Heaven-sent. Seeking treasure in the earth and seeking God in the sky were very much related disciplines to many of our forefathers.

To sum up: a con man named Winchell (or maybe Wingate) went from stealing a handful of coins to joining Priest Wood and trying to steal, in effect, the whole town.

Today, little remains to remind us of this strange and colorful episode. But I can't help recalling that the New Israelites, on orders from the St. John's Rod, began building a temple... until the rod changed its mind. So is it possible that somewhere in the wilds of Middletown Springs, or Tinmouth, or Wells, or Poultney, or Ira (the towns from which Middletown was carved) there may be the remains of that temple? We don't know exactly where it was or what it might have looked like. History's only clue is that it was later incorporated into the structure of a barn.

With the help of a dowsing rod, we could probably find it: a tumbled barn, a lost foundation, or maybe even a ghost. If not, then nothing remains of the New Israelites and the temple they almost built and a land that might have become the New Israel.

an AWFUL Story

"They didn't hurt us or anything, but I knew they were big enough to pick us up and carry us off. No doubt about it."
– Jim Guyette

An Awful Story

Irasburg, Vermont

Is there something weird in the air?

Flying saucers. Space junk. Drones. Meteors. Even a flying silo. The Vermont skies are busy with all sorts of Unidentified Flying Objects. But I don't believe there has ever been anything quite like what the Guyette family saw in the skies above Irasburg.

There, during one strange summer in the early 1980s, Jim Guyette encountered something soaring above the family farm. The incident started with an unearthly screech.

Not accustomed to such disturbances in the semi-isolated area, Jim dashed out to the porch to investigate. There he stood, looking up in wonder, not believing what he was seeing.

From inside the house young Ben Guyette heard his father's shout, "Come out here and look at this!" So, Ben and his brother ran outside. What they encountered could have been the subject of a horror movie.

Gigantic birds!

Or what seemed like birds.

"There were three of them," Ben said. "Me and my brother started walking out into the backyard, but my dad's yelling, 'Get back! They might pick you up!'"

They might pick you up? That's how big they were.

Jim, his wife Jeanette, their two sons, and a family friend all saw the colossal, winged wonders. They flew north in an unusual formation: two in front, one behind.

What could they have been? Not eagles, not hawks, not Canada Geese heading home. All five witnesses agreed the creatures were dark brown, possibly black, and sleek. They had long pointy heads,

87

long beaks, and elongated necks.

Jim estimated a wingspan of at least twenty feet from tip to tip. But, he said, there was something odd about those wings. "[They] were quite stiff-looking. They looked like bat wings, with a crick in them."

No one remembered any feet or legs, and, odder still, no feathers.

What happened next was every bit as extraordinary – the creatures vanished! "It was weird...." Ben told me. "You could see them plain as day, then all of a sudden they were just gone...."

His father added, "I didn't hear another sound. Didn't see a thing.... I don't know where they went."

In separate interviews, I asked both men what they *thought* they had seen. Ben didn't venture a guess, he just said, "It didn't look like any normal bird. I'd almost say it was prehistoric...."

His father was a little more speculative, "To me they looked like pterodactyl-things; they had that type of a head. And they were so huge...."

Pterodactyls in 1980s Irasburg? It doesn't seem very likely.

But if not, what are the other suspects? Are there, or have there ever been, gigantic, featherless bird-like things in Vermont? Were flying reptiles ever here, even in prehistoric times? Or could the Guyette family have been seeing something else, something perhaps a wee bit stranger?

To evaluate another possible suspect, we'll have to zoom over to Richford, which isn't very far away, only about 30 miles, as the pterosaur flies....

Richford, Vermont

Another horrifying airborne oddity has reportedly been darkening the skies of northwestern Vermont for, quite possibly, centuries. Known around Richford as simply *The Awful*, its first recorded sighting supposedly took place one evening in the early 1900s. Three men spotted it perched gargoyle-style atop the Boright building, right in the middle of town, at the juncture of Main and

River streets.

An old account describes it as looking like a Griffin, with two gray, 10-foot wings. A serpent-like tail adds 10-feet to its length. Its shriek and the sight of its nasty claws inspire instant terror. One of the first men to see it, a sawmill worker, was so petrified he had a heart attack on the spot. During his recovery he'd occasionally wake the household with his midnight screams.

Sometime after that, other locals spotted the flying monster soaring over the fields of Berkshire near the so-called "Lost Nation" area. Once the critter was observed with something clutched in its talons. Whatever it was struggled wildly and wailed like a baby. Some thought it was an infant, while others figured it was some small animal, like a lamb or piglet.

Oella Hopkins, the wife of a local farmer, was startled when her normally docile dog began barking fiercely. He seemed to be reacting to something overhead. She looked around from the laundry she was hanging. Something was perched on her porch roof, something hideous, glaring at her. Oella ran inside and hid under her bed, her dog right beside her. Sometime later she learned that others had also seen the loathsome creature, identifying it as *The Awful*.

The creature, whatever it may be, has allegedly put in occasional appearances ever since. According to H.P. Albarelli Jr.'s article in *The County Courier* (October 19, 2006), a new rash of 21st century sightings had begun.

Mr. Albarelli tells us that in early October 2006, "one of Richford's more solid citizens, a person who does not want to be identified in this article because 'people would think I've gone out of my mind,' reported seeing 'an unbelievable looking winged monster.'"

He watched in disbelief as the creature swooped down from on high and plucked a big black crow right out of the branches of a tree. "I didn't believe my eyes," the witness told the reporter, "but when the thing circled my house… well, then there was no denying it."

The same unidentified witness corroborated that stories of *The Awful* had been flying around for years. "I remember my grandfather once talking about that thing, but I thought it was just a story, a tall folk yarn," he told Mr. Albarelli. "What I saw was no yarn. Yarns don't fly and stories don't look like that. What I saw was real. And I hope to high heaven I never see it again."

Mr. Albarelli's article caused quite a stir in the community. Locals were alarmed to hear about their resident monster. Soon other newspapers and bloggers from all over the country – and even worldwide – had picked up the story. I was surprised to see the article reproduced in *The Fortean Times*, a glossy magazine published in England. Mystery mongers and legend trippers were on high alert. Queries flooded the small Enosburg Falls newspaper office.

What in hell was going on?

More Awful

Like a sequel to a horror movie, Mr. Albarelli's follow-up article appeared on November 30, 2006. He said the first article had encouraged more witnesses to speak up and, supposedly, enticed a flock of investigators to the area.

Lisa Maskell, who grew up in the vicinity, told *The County Courier*, "When I was about ten or eleven, we saw this thing sitting in a tree near the Trout River ... it was huge with large wings and a long, strange beak...." She reportedly said she thought it looked like a pterodactyl. "Big, scary, and fascinating."

"It's not a subject you want to talk to strangers or certain others about for good reasons," another unidentified local witness told the paper. "I didn't believe it at all at first," he said, "then some of us saw the thing a lot, some as recently as last month [October 2006], and the general feeling is we don't bother it and it don't bother us, maybe with a few exceptions."

Exceptions? So, it had bothered some people?

The witness failed to be explicit: "Let's just say a few animals have been lost to that thing."

At the end of his article in *The County Courier*, Mr. Albarelli concludes with a zinger that seems to promise another sequel: "Last week... this journalist was given a 'petrified jawbone' of 'one of these *Awful* creatures.' The partial jawbone, handed over by a Richford logger, is stone hard and bears a number of very large teeth."

Mr. Albarelli says he conveyed the relic to an expert animal biologist at the University of Vermont for identification.

Since then, there has been no follow-up article and no more publicly released information.

The Summary So Far

Okay, so what do we have here?

Reports of weird flying Whatzits ranging from Irasburg to Richford. In both cases the creatures make frightening sounds. Jim Guyette describes an unearthly screech. *The County Courier* witness talks about, "a pretty weird sound, like a low scream" and "when it gets closer, you can hear its wings, which sound like fat blankets being shook out."

At least two of the witnesses suggest the flyers resemble pterodactyls, which, science is convinced, are extinct flying reptiles, emphasis on *extinct*.

Are we dealing with two different critters? Or is the same airborne anomaly patrolling the skies all over northwestern Vermont?

Let's not jump to conclusions or ignore those nagging questions about misperception and deception. Then again, perhaps there is some tangible evidence: don't forget the petrified skull. But we'll come back to that.

The sum total so far is an alchemical hodge-podge that's far more than enough to keep us confused and guessing.

Yet, in his first *County Courier* article, Mr. H. P. Albarelli threw another mysterious log on the fire. He introduced the one character I have so far deliberately left out of this *Awful* saga. And I'm sure his name will be recognizable to most readers....

An Unexpected Cryptozoologist?

Those of us interested in the weirder aspects of New England – and especially Vermont – almost invariably cross paths with the renowned horror master from Providence, Rhode Island: the venerable H.P. Lovecraft. His fiction has influenced several generations of weird workers, myself included. But better-known scribes like the majestic Stephen King readily admit their debt to the esteemed HPL. An ever-growing list would also include Jorge Luis Borges, Joss Whedon, Neil Gaiman, and many more.

It is not important that we consider Mr. Lovecraft at length. The important things to keep in mind are the following:

1. He created a horrific cycle of myths involving elder gods who are trying to get us.

2. Although he wrote about the supernatural, he was in fact the consummate rationalist and didn't believe anything he wrote.

3. He was not a recluse, as he is often portrayed. He actually traveled a lot – including trips to Vermont.

4. In addition to writing fiction, he corresponded with an unbelievably vast quantity of people. (This last one is especially important.)

To this day the number of fans of his fiction is growing. But there is a sub-contingent of Lovecraft followers. In many cases they are people who have never taken the time to actually read his work. Nonetheless, they believe that what he wrote may not be entirely fiction. They believe there may really be ways to transcend the dimensions; there may, in fact, be elder gods waiting to destroy us lowly humans. It is all laid out, they say, in the dreaded *Necronomicon*, which might be a real book, if Mr. Lovecraft hadn't created it himself.

Mr. Alberelli's *Awful* article is a case where Mr. Lovecraft seems to have jumped from the fiction onto the non-fiction shelves.

The *Awful* article is presented as fact.

Mr. Alberelli begins, "In 1925, renowned horror writer H.P. Lovecraft secretly traveled to Richford and Berkshire [Vermont] to investigate a strange phenomenon that was occurring in the two towns. Lovecraft had been visiting friends in southern Vermont when he first learned about odd sightings [of *The Awful*] in Richford."

Now this is startling news to anyone who knows anything about H.P. Lovecraft. Could the skeptical Mr. Lovecraft have been a part-time paranormal investigator?

Unlikely but... possible.

But Mr. Albarelli goes on to say, "Locals [in the Richford area] were terribly afraid of a beast they had dubbed '*The Awful*.' According to records of old, [it] was a winged creature that resembled" – and here he quotes an unnamed source – "a very large Griffin-like creature with grayish wings that each spanned ten-feet."

The creature possessed "a serpent-like tail" and "huge claws that could easily grip a milk can's girth."

So, Mr. Albarelli is talking about a flying serpent with a 20-foot wingspan and a 10-foot tail. He says it's real, that it's stalking the skies of northwestern Vermont, and that H.P. Lovecraft went up there to investigate.

Okay, so now I'll investigate....

AUTHOR'S NOTES

At this point, being a Lovecraft fan and a chronicler of Vermont Folklore, my interest was really piqued. Here we have a local monster, far more sinister than Champ, and I'd never even heard of it! How could I have missed something this conspicuous? I figured I had to get to the bottom of things immediately.

First, I phoned Ethan Dezotelle, then editor of *The County Courier* newspaper, who assured me that the writer, Mr. H.P. Albarelli, is a real person with real publishing credentials. Apparently, he has a pretty far right political agenda, but I decided his politics don't seem relevant to the Awful saga.

Next, I examined the published story itself, looking for internal clues. Recall that Mr. Albarelli wrote that Mr. Lovecraft visited

Richford, Vermont, in 1925. The trip occurred while he was "visiting friends in southern Vermont."

Okay, maybe. But extensive research on Mr. Lovecraft fails to reveal that he had any friends anywhere in Vermont in 1925. It is documented, however, that HPL and his friend Paul Cook of Athol, Massachusetts, came to Vermont to visit the poet Arthur Goodenough of Guilford in August of 1927.

Then, in March 1928 and inspired by that 1927 visit, Mr. Lovecraft published an essay about his trip called *Vermont: A First Impression*.

A First Impression? We can reason that if he saw Vermont for the *first time* in 1927, he couldn't have been in southern Vermont and Richford in 1925.

The friends of record that he visited here were poet Arthur Goodenough in 1927, and entrepreneur, editor and Vermont secessionist Vrest Orton (founder of The Vermont Country Store) in 1928, after the Vermont Flood.

But as far as I know, no one has found any legitimate documentation that Mr. Lovecraft ever went monster hunting into northern Vermont. Or anywhere else.

Certainly, he was familiar with the writings of pioneering anomaly investigator Charles Fort, but HPL never showed any personal interest or belief in cryptozoology, the supernatural, or other "Fortean" phenomena. He was more likely to publicly debunk them.

Nonetheless, Mr. Albarelli writes, "When H.P. Lovecraft returned to southern Vermont from Richford he told friends [again unnamed] he was convinced that the Richford locals he had interviewed were" and here Mr. Albarelli directly quotes Lovecraft. [The locals were] "not in the least mistaken about what they had witnessed."

Supposedly Mr. Lovecraft later wrote – and this is said to be a direct quote – "The Awful became ample sustenance for my imagination" and "over time the creature became the basis for many of my own fictional inventions."

So, to be clear, Mr. Lovecraft is allegedly saying this Vermont creature inspired his Eldritch Tales. If so, where are those tales?

With a generous stretch of the imagination, could we postulate that *The Awful* might have inspired the Mi-Go in his only Vermont-based story, "The Whisperer in Darkness"? Probably not, they bear little, if any, resemblance.

Anyway, that was how Mr. Albarelli quoted Mr. Lovecraft. Trouble is, I can't find the quote anywhere I look. H.P. Lovecraft's life is one of the most thoroughly documented in literary history because of his voluminous correspondence – four published volumes of letters covering his life from 1925 until his death in 1937. Although it is nearly possible to pinpoint where he was and what he was doing on a given day, there is no mention of *The Awful* or his clandestine investigative journey to northern Vermont.

And – to be overly picky – one might be a little suspect of the diction. Granted, H.P. Lovecraft *could* be wordy, but the redundancy of saying "fictional inventions" seems a little over the top for a professional writer and editor.

There is also the peculiar use of the word "Griffin." Remember, Mr. Albarelli claims to have quoted an "old source" [that should read "old *unidentified* source"] that describes the Awful as looking like a Griffin. The word Griffin simply wasn't routinely used around here. Those critters make regular appearances in European legends. And the "old source" was not being usefully descriptive when it compared the appearance of one unknown animal to that of another unknown animal.

So finally, with my battery of suspicions intact, I contacted Mr. Albarelli himself. Essentially, I wanted to know just two simple things:

1. Is there a legitimate Vermont tradition of "Awful" sightings?

2. Is there any *proof* that H.P Lovecraft really ventured into northern Vermont in 1925?

Now I don't want to say Mr. Albarelli was evasive. I *will* say that Mr. Albarelli *seemed as if* he was being evasive.

He gave me the following information via email:

1. He had purchased an 1888 building in Richford. For years the building's top floor had been used as the local Masonic Temple. (*Ah-ha*! I thought, *a Masonic tie-in. The plot thickens!*)

2. There he found some interesting items, including several handwritten journals. In one he found a mention of *The Awful*. He didn't tell me whose journals they were.

3. He also found some original letters, all unpublished as far as he knows.

4. One of the letters, presumably penned by H.P. Lovecraft, supposedly validates his trip to Richford and his interest in *The Awful*. Mr. Albarelli says the letter is from Mr. Lovecraft to a Franklin Country minister and doctor, a friend of one of HPL's southern Vermont friends. He wouldn't name the doctor, the minister, or the friend, but Mr. Albarelli assured me the Lovecraft letter is quite genuine.

I have not seen the letter nor the journal. I was not invited to do so. Nor do I know of anyone who has seen the items in question.

I have not found a single scrap of evidence that suggests H. P. Lovecraft visited Vermont prior to 1927.

I can't find any indication *The Awful* existed in print or in the folk imagination prior to Mr. Albarelli's October 19, 2006, article in *The County Courier*. As far as I have been able to determine, his article contains the first-ever reference to *The Awful*.

So, what are we to make of all this?

The "Lovecraft as Cryptozoologist" business could be true, but I doubt it. It is not consistent with anything we know about the man.

For me it all comes down to a simple question: Is the Awful a real-life, three dimensional crypto-critter that stalks the forests and skies of northern Vermont? And by extension, is it the very same flying Whatzit that Ben Guyette saw in Irasburg and Lisa Maskell saw in Montgomery Center?

Or is it a "fictional invention" perpetrated by H.P. Lovecraft? Or H.P Albarelli? Or quite possibly. . . someone else? Maybe, but who? Some long-dead, Masonic, journal keeper and letter-writer?

Oh, and let's not forget that jawbone Mr. Albarelli turned over to the University of Vermont for identification. He told me in an email, "the UVM folks [again, unidentified] thought it was perhaps from sabre-tooth tiger."

Far as I know, those were not too plentiful around here, either.

MORE NOTES

I consulted with a number of people as I prepared this chapter. Perhaps the most Lovecraft-learned of the bunch was Donovan K. Loucks, Keeper of The H.P Lovecraft Archive (http://www.hplovecraft.com/).

Regarding Lovecraft as cryptozoologist: "Since Lovecraft described himself as a 'mechanistic materialist' – that is, a hardcore atheist – he wouldn't have bothered with any purported 'paranormal activity.'"

Mr. Loucks was kind enough to scan the extensive Archive of Lovecraft letters on my behalf, looking for clues. He said, "I searched through Lovecraft's extant letters for certain keywords like 'The Awful' and 'griffin' but found nothing noteworthy. Can you believe Lovecraft never refers to a griffin? I also searched for the town names of Richford and Berkshire... Not surprisingly, I found nothing."

And what about HPL visiting northern Vermont? "Lovecraft's visits to Vermont were confined to the Brattleboro and Guilford area. In fact, even though he mentions Newfane and Townshend in 'The Whisperer in Darkness,' he never saw these towns himself because the buses weren't running there the day he wanted to go!"

OH, AND ONE LAST THING...

Simply stated, I am convinced *The Awful* is a fabrication. Who's responsible? I'm not sure. I didn't do it, and neither did Mr. H.P. Lovecraft. Mr. H.P. Albarelli would be high on my list of suspects, but who can say for sure?

It might be worth pointing out that *The Awful* has some cousins that could have served as inspiration. In fact, there are stories of Awful-like flying monsters all over the country. A couple of examples will suffice:

The *Snallygaster* is said to darken the skies of Maryland and sometimes West Virginia, New Jersey, and Pennsylvania. It's described as a giant, flying bird-reptile hybrid with hooked claws, an enormous beak containing sharp teeth, and a ten-to-twenty-foot tail. Supposedly it has a terrifying screech but remains perfectly silent as it swoops down to carry off livestock or children. The legend is believed to have started in the early 1700s with German immigrant settlers. They called it a *Schneller Geist*, or "quick spirit." The name has evolved and so did descriptions of the creature. The legend, if not the creature itself, has apparently found its way beyond its original locale, and has flown all the way to Vermont.

Closer to home, there is the delightful legend of the "Giant Mosquito" of the White Mountains. Apparently "Giant Mosquito" was the Native American description of a massive bird-like critter that would appear like a thunderbolt out of a clear sky and carry off children or destroy their parents. It would deposit human and animal remains in its lair, a place called the "Devil's Den" on the face of Mount Willard. But who's to say its territory doesn't extend from the White Mountains all the way to northern Vermont?

MY CONCLUSIONS

Giant Mosquito = folktale

Snallygaster = folktale

The Awful = fiction

Guyettes' Sighting = Quite possibly true!

The Rutland Vermont Community Library

Extro

Before exiting this neighborhood of haunted houses and weird events, I want to be clear that this book was never intended to deny the existence of the supernatural. Weird things exist. Ghosts happen. And the "Vermont Ghost Experience" is, in fact, not confined to Vermont.

If I have taken a cautious stance, it is only because after years of study and investigation, I have become more cautious. We, as humans, have a longing for the divine. So, in consequence, it is only natural that we are often too quick to see the supernatural.

In these pages I have offered evidence for and against, and I tried not to overlook some exhibits that are simply unclassifiable. We can never reach a comfortable conclusion because the stories just keep coming. Any rules we may formulate are quickly neutralized by an apparent exception. As I state in the Foreword to Robert Brunelle's invaluable *The Lesser-Known Haunted Houses*, "I suspect [haunted houses] will continue to appear as long as carpenters keep erecting buildings and tenants continue to die in them."

So, I must reserve some enticing evidence for contemplation in future volumes, each of which, I predict, will demonstrate that our little state is far stranger than we might realize.

Let me conclude this book with a selection of cases in point. Previews of coming attractions, you might say.

For example, what are we to make of **The Rutland Vermont Community Library?**

To be sure, it houses "many a quaint and curious volume of forgotten lore…," but apparently it also houses… something else.

A long list of people – employees and patrons – have had baffling experiences there, experiences that simply cannot be explained. On the benign end of the weirdness continuum, books soar off the shelves, thud to the floor, then scuttle around like escaping animals. But on the other end, the library is one of the few haunted locations in Vermont where people actually see "ghosts." In period dress. Carrying on business as usual.

Could all this have anything to do with the three disused prison cells in the dark basement? Prison cells? Is Rutland too unforgiving when patrons are slow to return books? No, the building began life in the late 1850s as a United States Court House. You can imagine some of the evildoers who were detained there. Do the penitent spirits of murderers and book thieves lurk among the stacks?

Ransom Bay Inn

There are always tiny details that can make the skeptic's head spin. I found one during my visit to the Ransom Bay Inn in the Lake Champlain Islands at the intersection of Route 2 and Center Bay Road in Alburg. In its youth, while Washington was still President, it was a stagecoach stop. And I dare say great quantities of colonial rum and other spirits were consumed on site.

Now, I don't want to make this sound too spooky because this historic inn is a wonderful place to stay and enjoy a gourmet meal, a sound sleep, a sunny day, or a crashing storm off the lake. Amiable innkeepers Loraine and Rick will show you three original fireplaces, an old-fashioned wood cook-stove in the kitchen, beautiful antique furnishings, and a profusion of period details that give the impression that one might be free-floating in time. If the living can be temporally confused, what about any spirits that might linger in the old place?

When the owners began a massive renovation campaign, they seemed to disturb the unseen residents. Footsteps in an empty room or pacing on the stairs were disconcerting, but aggressively rattling door handles were terrifying enough to freeze the owners in their bed.

Guests sometimes found they couldn't re-enter their rooms because the doors had somehow been deadbolt-locked from inside. A tourist's photographs revealed the reflection of an unknown little girl in a guest's bedroom mirror.

But one unexpected visitation sent my imagination reeling. Two guests reported that they were awakened by "something" in their room. Opening their eyes, they both saw the same two presences staring down at them. But they were not the white filmy apparitions one normally associates with ghosts. Instead, they were ghostly black people, Africans. Unexpected. Out-of-place. And almost unheard of in local ghost lore.

A possible explanation occurred sometime later when a historian visited the inn. He was walking outside with Rick and Loraine when he noticed a triangular-shaped stone set into the chimney. It was the sign for "a safe house."

Suddenly the black ghosts and the secret room in the cellar all made sense. The inn had been a stop on the Underground Railroad.

It is difficult to explain this situation away: the ghosts were not simply a relic of the past, but they also revealed some history.

Loring G. Williams

I don't spend too much time thinking about reincarnation. The fact is it doesn't interest me very much. In all fairness, though, a book about the *Vermont Ghost Experience* would not be complete without a nod in that direction.

Simply put, reincarnation occurs when the spirit of a dead person comes back to earth, not to haunt a house, but to inhabit the body of a newborn baby, where it will begin life anew.

Such accounts would qualify as ghost stories, I suppose.

I have no idea about how many cases of reincarnation have been documented in Vermont, but in the mid-1960s Loring G. Williams, a teacher at the high school in Bellows Falls, was quite interested in hypnotism and Past Life Regression.

This process involves putting someone in a trance and enabling them to remember with remarkable clarity things that had happened in their distant past. Certain researchers claim that hypnosis can enable a person to access memories from more distant realms: lives that we have lived before.

Mr. Williams found an able subject in George Field, a 15-year-old high school student from Hinsdale, New Hampshire. During a hypnosis session George was instructed to remember what was going on prior to his birth. It was then that Jonathan Powell dropped in.

Jonathan said he had lived as a farmer in Jefferson, North Carolina, until he was murdered in 1863 by "damn Yankee soldiers." He had refused to sell them his potatoes, so they shot him in the stomach and left him to die in agony.

Unable to verify the many claims made in trance, Mr. Williams and George decided to head down to North Carolina to validate what they could. There George was regressed into Jonathan and was quizzed by the immensely skeptical town historian. Of the 25 people the historian mentioned, Jonathan recognized 15 and was able to fill in detailed information about their financial status, children's names, location of houses, relatives, and so on. A woman claiming to be Mr. Powell's great-grandniece said that her great-granduncle had been killed by Union solders exactly as described.

Well over 60 percent of George/Jonathan's information proved to be correct.

The saga is long and complicated and ultimately quite convincing. In a future book I'd like to dig into it more. Maybe I can find George Field himself. He was living in Hinsdale, New Hampshire, at the time. Possibly he is still there, or still around somewhere, contactable by phone, email, or hypnosis.

The Monk and the Mansion

It is rare in these stories that I can personally vouch for someone. However, this account comes from a very good friend who, time and again, has proven that she has an extraordinary memory. Because of her honesty and above-average recall, I include this as an authentic *Vermont Ghost Experience*.

But who, or what, was the ghost?

The events began near Rock Point, an undeveloped dagger of land extending into Lake Champlain, a little north of downtown Burlington.

It was 1969. Lily was 14 years old, small for her years, with blonde hair down to her waist and an irrepressible sense of adventure that propelled her through the surrounding forests and beaches as if she were a wood sprite.

On this particular summer day, she and her friend Nancy had decided to venture south across Rock Point and to visit "The Tables," a steep rock formation, perfect for congregating or 30-foot dives into the lake. "All the kids hung out there," she told me, "including those I thought were cute boys."

Lily remembers the trek through the woods seeming strangely long. She had a clear sense about the layout of the Rock Point promontory; she had been there many times. It was a straight shot −¬ north to south −¬ but things were just taking too long.

She felt momentary relief when she popped out of the woodland into a broad clearing. Then she looked around in confusion. By now, she thought, she should have reached the other side of the point. But there was no sign of the Tables nor the water's edge. And her friend Nancy wasn't with her anymore.

At the center of the clearing Lily saw an enormous castle-like building. The bare stone walls were stark in the afternoon sun, yet, in spite of the sunlight, the place looked shadowy, gothic, and surprisingly spooky. Surrounding it, here and there, grew a scattering of low trees.

Her immediate impression was that the building was vacant, yet as she approached, a man seemed to appear out of nowhere. He wore a long black robe, with no hood. She remembers a cord around the waist that hung down.

He looked but said nothing.

The contact had an uncanny feel to it. Lily recalls, "He sort of looked up, but it was like he ignored me. I was creeped out because I thought he was a monk and maybe he felt a young girl didn't belong on monastery grounds. But it was eerie. I really felt the urge to run. So, I bolted."

Moments later she was safely in the woods and quickly found her way to the Tables. "My friend was there too," she added. So, the girls just got back to their planned day, and everything was okay.

Lily never thought of the event as extraordinary until quite recently when she happened to find a photograph taken at about the time her 14-year-old self had seen the old building.

What she had witnessed on that long-ago summer afternoon was nothing like the building in the photograph. "Look there," she said, showing me things about the picture, "The trees around it are huge; they almost obscure it. And the building is nearly covered in ivy. It confuses me because this is so different from what I saw."

What Lily had seen – despite the shadows and gothic nuances – was a comparatively new structure. The trees were low and young. The walls were bare of vegetation.

Later she discovered another photograph, and the mystery deepened. It had been taken around 1850. This time things seemed eerily familiar. "I know that is definitely the place I saw," she told me, "but I know it can't be, too."

The building was erected in 1841 as Episcopal Bishop John Henry Hopkins's residence. In 1854 it became a theological seminary. Fire claimed it in 1979; it was torn down some time after that. So, it still existed when Lily saw it. But when she saw it, it looked the way it had appeared a century before.

So, what was really happening here? At first glance the entire episode might seem like the imaginings of a lost little girl. But as I said at the start, I trust Lily's memory and consider this story – as our Roman Catholic friends might say – "worthy of belief."

To recap: Lily, it seems, stepped through a curtain of trees and into another era. In 1969 she saw a building and a clergyman as they were, circa 1850.

We can only speculate about what was happening on the other end of the continuum. Did she manifest as an apparition to a bewildered holy man at the midpoint of the 19th century? Could he have perceived the child with blonde waist-length hair as a religious visitation? Did he record the event in some undiscovered diary that may yet come to light?

Or was it destroyed in the 1979 fire? If so, this mystery, like so many others, will remain unsolved and unsolvable.

Each of the stories in this chapter has unique qualities that make them especially fascinating for me. A library, supposedly the repository of all knowledge, exists synchronously with an ongoing mystery that none of its books can explain. A unique chimney design reveals details about a building's past and the solution to a "ghost story." A New England boy exhibits uncanny recollections about historic Civil War events, and a little girl – for no discernible reason – has a random vision of the past.

The "Why" of all this will fuel myriad discussions. Strange stories will continue to accumulate. I'll fill another book with *Vermont Ghost Experiences*. And all the mysteries will prove too vexing to solve in a single lifetime.

About the Creators

AUTHOR

Joseph A. Citro is Vermont's resident expert on unexplained phenomena and bizarre historical events. A native Vermonter, he has authored 15 books, lectured widely, and appeared on regional and national radio and television. His books include *Passing Strange* and the folk horror novel *Shadow Child*.

ARTIST

Robert Waldo Brunelle Jr. is a 7th generation Vermonter. He is a painter, illustrator, kinetic sculptor, art educator, and creator of the political cartoon strip *Mr. Brunelle Explains It All*. His books include *The Useful Object Factory*, *The Lesser Known Haunted Houses*, and *The Vermont Ghost Experience* (with Joe Citro).

Made in the USA
Columbia, SC
05 October 2021